SPIRITUAL DISCERNMENT AND POLITICS

J. B. Libânio

SPIRITUAL DISCERNMENT AND POLITICS

GUIDELINES FOR RELIGIOUS COMMUNITIES

Translated from the Portuguese by
Theodore Morrow

Reproduced by permission of
Orbis Books

Wipf and Stock Publishers
EUGENE, OREGON

The Catholic Foreign Mission Society of America (Maryknoll) recruits and trains people for overseas missionary service. Through Orbis Books Maryknoll aims to foster the international dialogue that is essential to mission. The books published, however, reflect the opinions of their authors and are not meant to represent the official position of the society.

Wipf and Stock Publishers
199 West 8th Avenue, Suite 3
Eugene, Oregon 97401

Spiritual Discernment and Politics
Guidelines for Religious Communities
By Libanio, J.B.
Copyright© January, 1977 Orbis Books
Print date: January, 2003
Previously published by Orbis Books, January, 1977 .

To the memory of my old provincial superior,
Father John-Bosco Penido Burnier,
in gratitude for the heroic testimony of martyrdom
in the service of justice and charity

Contents

Introduction 1

PART ONE
PREREQUISITES FOR DISCERNMENT 5

Chapter I
Submitting to a Process of Purification 7
    From Individual to Socio-Dialectical Consciousness   7
    "Position" as a Source of Inordinate Affections   11
    Questioning Our Social Position   14

Chapter II
Generosity 19
    Committing Our Best Efforts   19
    The True Field of Generosity   20
    The Social Position of the Poor   21
    Privileged Position in the Church and in the Religious Life   22

Chapter III
Prayer 26
    Prayer as Clarification of Faith   26
    Prayer as Stimulation of Hope   27
    Prayer as Purification of Charity   29
    Summary   30

PART TWO
STRUCTURE OF THE ACT OF DISCERNMENT 31

Chapter IV
The General Intention 33
    The Traditional Schema   34
    The Historical Schema   35

    The Frailty of Our Knowledge   36
    The "Gospel Universal"   36
    The Paths of Charity   37
    A Utopian Project   38
    The Concept of Justice   38

Chapter V
Concrete Mediation   *44*
    Mediation as Kenosis   44
    Politics   45
    Analysis of Reality   46
    Choice of Instrumentality   50
    Four Levels of Analysis   52
    Analysis of Our Personal Circumstances   59
    Escape from Mediations   65
    Mediations and Their Exigencies   68
    Summary   73

Chapter VI
Types of Discernment   *75*
    The Intuition of the Mystic and the Prophet   75
    The Doubt and Anxiety of "Existentialists"   78
    The Reasoning Faith of "Logical Thinkers"   81
    Relationships of Faith and Politics   84
    Summary   91

PART THREE
CRITERIA FOR DISCERNMENT   *93*

Chapter VII
Subjective Criteria   *95*
    Potentialities of the Subject   95
    The Existence of Support Structures   96
    Internal Composure   104

Chapter VIII
Objective Criteria   *106*
    The Theological Dimension   106
    The Christological Dimension   109

 The Ecclesiological Dimension 118
 Summary 121

Conclusion *123*

Notes *127*

SPIRITUAL DISCERNMENT AND POLITICS

Introduction

Our lives are caught up in a lacerating tension between the forceful drive for unity and totalization on the one hand and, on the other, the multidimensionality of life in the concrete, of unpredictability, of incompleteness, of diversity. The search for unification may enter into our life as truth or as falsehood, as freedom or as oppression, as a gradual process or as a sudden imposition. There are two areas where this penchant for unity is most clearly evident: in religion (dogma) and in politics (ideology).

"Unification of the truth is at once the wish of reason and a first violence, a fault. We shall thus reach a point of ambiguity, a point of greatness and of guilt."[1] Politics and religious faith are the realm of the "unification of truth," thus falling subject to the danger of ambiguity between "the exercise of reason" and "a first violence." The purpose of this book is to attempt an illumination of the relationship between politics and the inspiration provided for us in the reading of the Christian scriptures. This will not follow the classic approach, in general terms, to the theme of "faith and politics," but will approach the subject from the perspective of *spiritual discernment*.

There is a long tradition in the spirituality of the church that has analyzed and continues to analyze the experience of trying to discover the will of God through the innumerable concrete situations that confront us. We have a choice among innumerable possibilities for serving God, for constructing the kingdom of God in history. Spiritual discernment seeks to be of assistance in making these choices, proceeding from a vision of faith.

The present work has as a thematic presupposition a more detailed work on the essential structure of discernment, which we hope to complete in the very near future. Here we shall be dealing with the problems of discernment in relation to a context wider than the individual's personal search for the will of God. We want to see what assistance can be derived from this spiritual tradition in the choice of concrete procedures in the political realm.

We are at once confronted with a basic difficulty. Is it possible that the spiritual process of discernment, which during its long tradition was more often utilized at the individual level to assist persons in finding their proper vocation among the various concrete alternatives of life, could be considered as a program for some external sphere of activity, such as the choice of political measures? Are these not two different fields, and does not spiritual discernment pertain to the individual level, whereas politics belongs to the sphere of the *polis*, the city?

Spiritual discernment is an ascetic practice that seeks to discover the will of God—that is, a way of incorporating love, concrete charity, into our lives. We can say without equivocation that social justice is one of the more privileged works—mediations—of charity. And politics is in turn the privileged field for the realization of justice. Thus it would seem that politics is a privileged field for discernment.

Politics relates basically to power. Power, in turn, is the locus where one finds demonstrated most clearly both the greatness and the depravity of human nature. It is the instrument of the historical rationality of the body politic. Its scope is enormous. This means that a vast reserve is available either for service and justice or for exploitation and injustice. It is the political existence of humankind that gives sin its historical and social dimensions, its destructive power, and its breadth. Power has a way of revealing the deep-rootedness of sin, just as it can also reveal the heroism of devotion to the common good. It uncovers the true root of sin, which is not pleasure but the arrogant desire for dominion, the turpitude of covetousness, of oppression.[2]

Hence the importance of introducing into this sphere, concerned as it is with politics and with power, the richness of experience that comes from spiritual discernment. What I have written should be thought of as an experimental venture, a rough draft in a field where this approach is relatively new. Its tentativeness will be in evidence throughout the book, as I attempt to incorporate elements that Christians engaged in the process of liberation have been working out on the basis of their political experience in conjunction with the inspired tradition of the Christian scriptures.

The French bishops, when grappling with the subject of "Christians and politics," have reminded us that an effort should be made for enlightenment and discernment, if the aspiration to bring about a more just and more comradely society is not to be subverted en route, but is on the contrary to benefit from humanity's positive evangelical impulses.[3] In the political context especially, discernment must receive our attention. In concluding their document, they suggest the following as fundamental attitudes for the Christian to have in the present world situation: seriousness, enlightenment, determination, and imagination. Discernment means precisely a search for enlightenment,

INTRODUCTION

which in turn calls for determination and imagination in a serious taking of responsibility in proportion to the scope of actions that are judged to be either accepted or rejected.

The purpose of our reflections in this work is to provide coordinates for Christians, especially members of religious orders or congregations, to orient themselves, from the Christian standpoint, to the complex problem of choosing political programs. We are trying to map out directions that could help to free us from ideological preconceptions, cloaked in religious overtones, that could prove to be blinkers on our vision. The interest that motivates us derives from a praxis of liberation, one of whose concerns is to create the circumstances that will unmask the true position of conservative ideologies. Questions raised at the ideological level will be important to the extent that they are related to praxis. The basic thing is not discernment, not some new perception of reality, but a change in that reality, such that our new consciousness is "veri-fied"—"made true"—in concrete reality, and this is what is expressed in our consciousness. The basic interest is to transform a situation that, interpreted in the light of divine revelation, is shown to be counterevangelical. The process of discernment is but a small contribution to the interpretation of this reality in the light of divine revelation, using the key of faith. Improving the reading process or contributing a key of interpretation will be to no avail if change does not take place in objective reality. It is of no use to discern the will of God in actions that attempt to deal with the contradictions and conflicts of society if these actions do not change history by their application to it.

It is within this view of things, and on the basis of this underlying interest—which will be assumed as the basic and prerequisite viewpoint in this work—that what is written in these pages is to be understood. It is an unpretentious, soft-spoken message within the vast prophetic stream that is now pouring over the Latin American church. It awakens "the Christian hope that points toward a new humanity, reconciled with itself and brought into kinship with the universe . . . and it calls for a relentless, active presence capable of calling forth within the flow of history the signs of the resurrection and the identifying features of the new humanity of the future."[4]

The structure of the work is simple. In Part One we attempt to elaborate the prerequisites for spiritual discernment in political matters. The first prerequisite is to be located within the *process of purification*, which is manifested in overcoming a purely individualistic consciousness, moving in the direction of a dialectico-social perception, and exercising a critical vigilance with respect to one's own social position (Chap. I). The second prerequisite is the attitude of *generosity*, as expressed in the Ignatian ideal of the "more" (*magis*). This generosity finds special expression in relation to one's choice of social position as an expression of concern for the oppressed, with or without an actual sharing of experiences with them, or possibly even a more radical "incarnation" in their environment (Chap. II). The third prerequisite is a climate of *prayer* as a "clarifier" of faith, an activator of hope, and a purifier of charity (Chap. III).

Part Two is the central corpus of the work. Here we seek to study the *structure of the act of discernment*. It consists basically in the dialectical relationship between a "general intention" (Chap. IV) to seek the will of God in our own socio-politico-historical context and the concrete mediations (Chap. V) that express God's will in such a context. Our analysis seeks to clarify the meaning of such a "general intention" in the process of discernment, which includes the taking of choices from the socio-political spectrum. We shall also concern ourselves with a better understanding of what is meant by "concrete mediation" and the various steps we must take in discerning the choice to be made (Chap. VI).

Part Three is concerned with providing aids in establishing *criteria for discernment*. First we deal with the subjective aspects of the discerning process (Chap. VII). We then attempt to show how objective criteria help us to form our decisions. These are presented in three dimensions: the theological, the christological, and the ecclesiological (Chap. VIII).

The Conclusion takes up again the question of the magnitude and complexity of politics and how we can understand it through the approach of faith. Faith does not exempt us from risk or from responsibility. It does offer us help in making our decisions. And all that we hope to accomplish is to demonstrate the importance of a critical vigilance over the political sector and of the function of faith. If the reader, when finishing the work, understands that we are confronting a basic reality that requires of us a major critical commitment in the name of our responsibility as Christians and as religious, we can look for a more enlightened and committed action in building up the kingdom. The primary thing that interests us is not the ideas presented here. What is all-important is the kingdom of God, the "one thing necessary." In light of this, any work of ours, any effort, any struggle, any commitment is beside the point. For the Lord left us, as a summary of his own life work, the serious imperative: "Set your mind on God's kingdom and his justice before anything else, and all the rest will come to you as well" (Matt. 6:33).

PART ONE

PREREQUISITES FOR DISCERNMENT

Every process has its necessary preconditions; if they are not observed, it cannot be set in motion without running the risk of profound deformation. On the matter of personal spiritual discernment, St. Ignatius alerts us to the need of a purification as an indispensable condition for viewing facts and the course of history to discern the presence of the Absolute who calls us into question. In his religious vocabulary, Ignatius uses the expression "quitarse las afecciones desordenadas"—*to eliminate our inordinate affections.*

Chapter I

Submitting to a Process of Purification

The problem may be posed as follows: When exercising spiritual discernment concerning a political situation that is not primarily spiritual, what does it mean to submit to a process of purification? What are the factors that keep us from possessing a clear vision, and what is it that radically perverts any discernment relating to something of a political nature? Are they the same factors as those that traditional religious practice has always spelled out? Or is there, because of the nature of the matter, a kind of "inordinate affection" within the very person who believes that he or she is spiritually detached, which somehow evades the jurisdiction of the ascetic practices imposed? Could there be factors that unduly influence a person in the political field, so that an individual spiritual approach to detachment is not enough? And could decisions made in this way be well intended as far as the individual's conscience is concerned, and yet not be in alignment with the building up of the kingdom of God in history? Does the kingdom of God have concrete, objective requirements that go beyond the level of individual spiritual awareness?

These questions lead us to a series of reflections on the factors that interfere with human judgment in political matters, and how they are to be dealt with.

From Individual to Socio-Dialectical Consciousness

All the questions raised presuppose a change in the horizon of one's understanding, without which it is impossible to comprehend the entirety of the problem treated in these pages. This change is characterized basically by a dialectical comprehension of individual consciousness as it relates to the social realm. In the cultural tradition that is very precious to members of the church and those following the religious life, so much primacy is attributed to individual consciousness that the social dimension may well be neglected. Good intentions are given precedence, the desire to do good is encouraged, good wishes are in high esteem, to the extent that the individual appears as a person situated on an island of freedom, threatened by temptations that seek to overcome him or her. For all practical purposes, importance is attached only to a person's determination to be faithful, combined with an awareness illuminated by the principles of correct doctrine and sound morality. From this standpoint, all that is needed is conversion of heart, and the problems are solved.

This way of thinking corresponds to a traditional way of viewing Christian life. Sacramental and moral practices are stressed as an expression of this "conversion of heart." And so we have mission and preaching in line with the slogan, "Save your soul." The renewal movement directly deriving from Vatican Council II did not radically change this viewpoint. True, it did criticize the superficial nature of many "conversions." It questioned the superficiality involved in them because of the insistence on external features of religious practice that left the depths of the heart untouched. This viewpoint adopted by the council retained, however, the basic feature that conversion of heart is the source of all changes in society and that it must be related to pastoral activity.

To give an example of this modern expression of pastoral ministry, we could mention the Cursillo movement. The analysis of O. Dana shows us how there exists in the pastoral vision of the Cursillo movement the clear presupposition that the central problem is conversion of the individual and that any other change derives from it:

> Through it all is seen the conception of life viewed from the standpoint of grace—which does not consist in *doing* this or that but in *being* a child of God, a brother or sister of Christ, and a living temple of the Holy Spirit, and, in acting in this capacity, all problems will be radically solved....
>
> We can be quite certain that a new world is in preparation. A new generation is rising up, convinced that renewal must begin with individuals in order subsequently to reach institutions.... Lay persons who reform their own mentality and bring their life into accord with the image of Christ... acting fully on their own responsibility, transform

the temporal structures in which they are immersed, guided by their vision of Christ remaking the world from its very foundations, transforming it from savage to human, from human to Christian, and then into the kingdom of God. . . .

The originality of the Christian message does not consist in a direct affirmation of the necessity for changing structures, but in the insistence that we be committed to the conversion of the individual, who urgently requires this transformation.[5]

This is the same line taken by youth movements and practically all pastoral movements today. They are looking for a conversion of heart, with the hope that, beginning here, other changes will be made. Catholic colleges and universities are training a Catholic elite, so that its members, with their Christian education, will then change society.[6]

This conception of an intimist, individualistic faith, as a reality that transforms the human heart, cherishes the hope that other changes will come about in consequence. If, however, we make our approach from the standpoint of the "theology of liberation," which is the position that we are taking in this work, then the above viewpoint will seem *woefully naive*. Have we not experienced four centuries of the predominance of this viewpoint in Latin America and the sad, painful fact of confrontation with profoundly unjust structures that have been brought about and maintained—or at any rate have not been changed—by the Christian ruling class? The process of discernment in this perspective will be restricted to those currents that aim at changing the individual and leaving the structures intact.

Another determining factor in this conception is the importance of elaborating a doctrinal and moral orthodoxy of a universal and definitive nature, as a source of clarification and enlightenment for Christian life. Discernment is thus situated within the field of orthodoxy, in such a way that external reality seems to be directly and immediately understood as the object of the principles of correct action. Individuals perceive themselves as confronting that reality, armed with a rule that is predetermined and preestablished, according to which they are to orientate their activity.

Such an understanding of discernment makes a number of false assumptions. Foremost among these is that the individual is simply standing in front of reality, as if in a position "outside" reality, whence a judgment be made. But this is the emplacement proper to God, who is immanent and transcendent in time and space. And this is the great temptation of human beings wanting to be like God (Gen. 3:5), to be in that nongeographical locus from which they can unmask all reality to the point of full illumination and clarity, thus enjoying total clairvoyance in decision-making. Obviously, only an overpowering delusion could permit anyone to see things thus. Humankind is *in* the situation, not *in front of* it. This means that the situation, reality, has a decisive influence on the human condition, touching and shaping it.

Reality is molded by human beings and it in turn molds them. There are two extremes that misrepresent the true process of history: that a person makes history to such an extent that history depends on his or her goodwill, on his or her intentions, on his or her goodheartedness; or that history is so deterministically regulated that the human role is reduced to that of a mere puppet. A dialectical understanding permits us to see reality in a more nuanced perspective. Everything that exists in society, all existing social relationships, are human creations. There is no suprahuman power forging human and social realities. All are the work of human beings. On the other hand, as humankind externalizes and objectifies its creations and structures and interpersonal relationships, they begin to leave their mark on the persons they contact, they begin to determine and condition them. All change passes through the mediation of this reality. On the person who has thus been determined, new changes will have their impact.

In short, individual consciousness acts upon a reality that acts upon it. From this standpoint it is a mistake to conceive of discernment as a mere application of universal principles on the part of an impartial, purely judgmental consciousness. Individual consciousness is that of a player who judges from within the game, not that of a referee outside the game with the rule book, making decisions on plays in which he or she takes no personal interest.

The acquisition of a dialectical consciousness of social reality is indispensable if there is to be any possibility of discernment. We must get away from the deceptive illusion of an impartiality that never existed. Ideological commitments were thought to be neutral because of an unawareness of the dialectical situation. It was thought that the *wish* to be neutral was the same as *being* neutral. One had the impression that the decision of individual consciousness to be free of preconditioning was all that was needed to ensure that such preconditioning did not exist. All the while, a deep-rooted idealism was at work.

Nondialectical consciousness tends to make another mistake. The individual thinks that he or she is perceiving reality directly. In fact, what is said and understood is from within the pattern of an ingenuous interpretation that is usually popularized by the dominant ideology. The smug certainty of having grasped reality itself through the perceptiveness of one's own principles never gets beyond a naive acceptance of the prevailing interpretation; because persons do not recognize the mediating factor between them and reality, they cannot criticize it. One cannot be critical of something of which one is unaware. And the unknown factor in this case is the very ideological position in which one is caught up, a position that profoundly determines one's discernment, inasmuch as one feels that the action taken is based entirely on one's clear understanding and free will. The seemingly obvious concepts run the risk of having no content other than what has been assigned to them by the prevailing or dominant ideology.[7]

"Position" as a Source of Inordinate Affections

Within the context of individualistic spirituality, we may include in the category of inordinate affections the various types of attachment to comfort, pleasures, selfish individual interests, and the like. Their control is seen in an ascetic detachment, a doing battle with (*agere contra*) our sensual nature. In line with the thoughts expressed in the previous section of this chapter, a new source of such affections emerges: "social position."

All of us are part of a huge chess game, participating in a conflict between social forces. Society is not some harmonious entity afflicted with only minor disfunctions in the process of being corrected, as adherents of the functionalist school assume. They give preeminence to the idea of an order where social equilibrium is disturbed only by some malfunctioning of the component parts. Such a conception of reality favors an illusion that leads to unrealistic, quixotic schemes aimed at dealing with structural conflict at the level of its apparent disfunctioning. A paternalistic pastoral approach that labors to reconcile social classes on the basis of some kind of sympathetic mutual acceptance, but which fails to change the mechanisms that generated their alienation, will never be more than a palliative. This is like treating a fever derived from an infection while leaving the infection intact.

A dialectical approach makes central to the comprehension of society the concept of conflict, of tension, of struggle, where opposing interests clash. Power is related to interest groups. Each of us has a position that relates to conflict. This social position influences our perception of the problems, our evaluation of the situation, our manner of grasping the values involved, and our prioritizing them into a hierarchy. Our social position is characterized above all by our social praxis. This in turn is defined by the interests that it supports. When there are conflicts of interest, neutrality is impossible. Abstention will always be a vote for something. The overall effect of our human actions is involved in the process of transforming the world; this is a social matter because it converges with the interests of some group or social class. Once we have become situated in history, it is impossible for us not to occupy a position. Our actions line up with certain predetermined interests prevailing in the society, or else line up against them. This social position is closely tied to the place where we live and work, to the person to whom we relate, to the commitments and communities of interest that we form, and to the ideological subordinations and alliances that we establish. Our social position permits certain views and activities, and prohibits others.[8]

Our social praxis is constituted by the totality of our educational, economic, theoretical, ideological, and political activities. This is a profoundly decisive factor in all of our choices, all of which take place within that praxis, not outside it. To be more concrete, we could say that a province of a religious order or a religious community that has a certain location (habitation) and that maintains relations with persons and interests of the dominant class lacks the prerequisites for spiritual discernment with regard to political reality. It will be influenced by this "inordinate ideological affection," so that its decision-making will not allow it to comprehend reality in a socio-analytical manner (seeing), in order to evaluate it from a critical perspective (judging), and then do something about it (acting). These judgments will be strongly corrupted by the equivocations absorbed at earlier stages.

The ideological outreach of such a community or province may be so extensive that all the spiritual energies generated in retreats and "conversions" serve only to accelerate the rhythm of dedication and even of personal renunciation, without at the same time criticizing and correcting the interests that incarnate the ideology. The overarching delusion here is that a province or community can be renewed by spiritual means. The whole process of renewal is perverted by false views of reality projected by the ideological position in which it is situated. Its social position, especially for more intellectual groups, provides an enormous potential for rationalization, which in turn provides reinforcement for the idea of not changing anything.

The ideology of the social position in which a person stands is so all-encompassing that its adherents fail to see the reality beyond it. Unless a break is made with such a position, spiritual discernment is impossible. This ideology exerts at the group level the same sort of influence that selfishness and sensuality introduce into personal acts of discernment. St. Ignatius, as a precondition for discernment, makes the individual level the locale for the battle against one's own sensuality, the making of a decision to detach oneself from the object of one's inordinate affections (*Spiritual Exercises,* n. 155).

For our purposes, the Ignatian intuition will be translated into the following terms. Only by setting aside the social position committed to the dominant ideology will it be possible for us to realize the prerequisite for an act of discernment, an apostolic sounding of a given province or community. It is more common for such soundings to be taken from within the "inordinate" situation. We cannot expect much from such probings. They serve only to confirm the situation, at best improving certain personal attitudes but quite ineffective in dealing with the larger context.

Ideology performs the function of a pragmatic theory—corresponding to spirituality in the field of personal discernment—that keeps alive the system to which one is committed. Efforts are made to bring together the maximum number of possible elements, resulting in a complex of principles and values, to justify, confirm, and activate the system in question. Ideology is not concerned with truth but with its own practical functioning. It appropriates the truths and self-manifestations of the social body that it dominates, so as to gain greater penetration and efficacy. The more the values of this system are threatened, the greater will be the effort of the ideologues to defend it with arguments that are, if not true, at least plausible. The contents of the arguments are not important in that they have the force of truth, but only to the extent that they justify the interests in question. Many acts of discernment by religious communities and provinces fall into error precisely because the arguments pro and con represent a search, not for truth, but for their own interests. They are backed up by emotional and ideological arguments.

Social position is the determining factor in this game. The more the members of the community or province are inclined to intellectual and ideological discussions, the more difficult it will be to break out of this circle. Theological and religious arsenals will yield a multitude of highly convincing arguments. Their proponents forget, however, that theological and religious truth has quite a different function. They are not seeking the truth but a confirmation of interests defined by the social position in which they find themselves. The ideology, because it is so important to the persons doing the discerning, comes up with a maximum of religious motivations to justify the dominant interests. They read the scriptures and the traditions of the church in such a way that their social position is only reinforced, because the social position is their point of departure.

What is missing in this type of discernment—a fundamental flaw—is brought out by the question already raised as to its underlying motivation: What social position is the starting point for this discernment? Is this social position appropriate for making an evangelical act of discernment? Are we not obligated to first change the social position in order to initiate a process of discernment that would give us some minimum guarantee that we are reading history in the light of the faith? Thus the problem revolves around the following: How, if we are in such a social position, are we going to question it, especially if this position is nurtured by the dominant ideology in which it is encapsulated?

Questioning Our Social Position

This question brings us to some thoughts on the possibility of socio-dialectical consciousness.[9] A social group will never come to the point of questioning its social position if the larger civil or religious society in which it finds itself has been unresponsive to the impact of change. A society—in our case the church, or the religious congregation, province, or community—that is ensconced within the established order, is hardly aware of any threats to itself, and is satisfied with itself, does not present to its members the possibility of developing a consciousness oriented toward change. The church or a religious congregation or community can realize this state of pure tranquility only within a stable society—or as the victim of an extreme alienation from changes in society. In the latter case, it is difficult to carry on for any length of time in today's world. It is practically impossible for any religious group to live totally alienated from radical social changes.

In other words, it is possible to have a consciousness oriented to change in the social position of a group when society is undergoing changes and is not in a stationary, self-satisfied condition. Restlessness, dissatisfaction, the perception of a lack of essential values and of meaning in existent structures are the factors that promote a possible change in social position. And these elements are now at work. For twenty years now, it has been utterly impossible for the religious life in Brazil to shrug off suspicions as to the social position in which its members are living.

It is quite evident to everyone that we live in a society profoundly stirred by ideological movements that seek to change it and others that seek to keep it within a predetermined pattern of interests. It is a propitious moment for raising questions. What preconditioning is necessary before a society can begin to question itself? How can these questionings of society get through to the group of religious that is seeking to exercise discernment as to its apostolic activities?

A group finds itself moving in a circle, kept in motion by an interaction between ideology and praxis. The group lives out a praxis that is justified and reinforced by an ideology. It lives out an ideology that is confirmed and concretized in its praxis. This circling tends to perpetuate itself, given the force of the interaction between ideology and praxis. History may go its own way with its serious problems, its restlessness and anxieties and questionings, but the group keeps circling around its poles of praxis and ideology, oblivious to the questionings of society. There is one circle touching on two levels: the level at which reality is analyzed and the level at which the faith is understood. And these two levels are represented as reflections of each other.

Praxis, with its corresponding ideological understanding of reality, conditions the interpretation of the faith and of Christian praxis. These in turn, moving in a circle, confirm praxis and the interpretation of reality. On the one hand, there is an interpretation of the faith conditioned by one's view of reality and on the other there is a view of reality nurtured by one's interpretation of revelation. An intertwining takes place between faith and reality, between ideology and practice, keeping the religious group insulated from any questioning of that view.

Such a situation can begin to be questioned only if two suspicions arise with regard to it: Could this view (ideology) of reality and the actions that grow out of it (praxis) be falsified at their roots? Could it be that the interpreter of revelation, precisely because of his or her false understanding of reality, has also distorted the meaning of revelation? The initial stage of questioning is *suspicion*. It is more than simply a doubt. It is an insight, still dim and unconfirmed but already charged with an interrogatory force. This suspicion is translated for the most part by a series of questions concerning the meaning of the praxis and of the theory (ideology) that justifies it, as also concerning the interpretation of revelation and religious practice. The more abundant and radical and far-reaching these questions, the more serious becomes the suspicion and the less easily it can be dismissed.

Moving on in our analysis, we find still another question raised: What, after all, prompts us to raise questions as to our way of viewing reality and our way of acting upon it? What is the source of this suspicion? How is it that at a certain moment we entertain a suspicion concerning an understanding of reality and social practice that always seemed beyond question until now? What is it that arouses suspicion? Is it possible to elicit suspicions? To create them? How?

The source of suspicion is experience, a new praxis in terms of what has come before, such that the former praxis and its corresponding theory (ideology) come under suspicion. Here we have a *new way of experiencing reality*. An innovation has disturbed the order of things. The novelty of the experience awakens a latent dissatisfaction with the way we have lived until now. This new experience has to be encountered in terms of what actually makes it original or different, or raises questions about a prior identification. This experience might be a contact made with some critical group that questions our own actions, that shakes our confidence in the data we possess, that unmasks our ideologies. Or it could be a painful direct contact, over a period of time, with some distressing social reality. For many groups of religious, a direct apostolic experience shared with persons who are suffering is the source of profound changes, derived from the suspicions that this experience arouses. For others, access to new theological insights of a more social nature was a dramatic enough experience to arouse suspicion with regard to their prior social activity. In fact, there are a vast number of possibilities for an experience to be the first stage of a suspicion.

We must not delude ourselves: these are the conditions under which a change is possible; they are not themselves the change. It could be cancelled out by any number of factors. But without such a suspicion, the possibility for change cannot follow. Suspicion may be raised, new questions may be posed—and the religious group may go on without changing its interpretation of reality or of the faith. The process that makes change possible has been interrupted. In order to go forward, there must be a search for a new interpretation of reality and of revelation. This new interpretation permits an encounter with new knowledge by shedding light on a new praxis that is to be instituted. Then we have a new circle: theory and praxis in relation to reality; theory and praxis in relation to revelation. This circle can then be closed or can be allowed to remain open indefinitely to new experiences, to new suspicions, and, above all, to the possiblility of new changes. Thus the process continues.[10]

Digging deeper into this line of thought, we may still ask: What permits a group to have a new experience, such that it could arouse their suspicions with respect to their own theory and practice, when so many others have experiences that do not arouse the least suspicion? Sometimes two groups will have similar experiences, and one will begin to question while the other remains inflexible in its earlier position.

To use a psycho-sociological interpretation, we may say that the self-confidence of the group is at issue in these experiences. One group, feeling itself threatened to submit to questioning, resists. The group becomes rigid, confusing its identity in a given historical moment with the only possibility of self-perpetuation. But another group opens itself to questioning and permits the otherness of the experience to test it. In other words, there are psycho-social mechanisms that act in either one direction or another. But we cannot reduce everything to psychological mechanisms. Revelation can also assist us in interpreting such an event.

There are no mechanisms that deterministically bring a group to a genuine conversion, conducting it through the stages of suspicion, fresh analysis, and a new understanding of reality to a new praxis. A more structured presentation, such as we have made thus far, is not intended to downplay a basic attitude of *openness* as a prerequisite condition for self-questioning. In its theological dimension, this openness entails an awareness of "the other" in the search for my salvation. In any situation that I might encounter, I am not saved without the mediation of the other, of that which is different. An attitude of self-satisfaction, of profound contentment and complacency with myself, excludes me from the very possibility of salvation. This necessitates a permanent attitude of openness to the new, to the other, to the different, as a requirement for being Christian. God is the Other, the not-I. This dimension of faith is the basic condition to be fulfilled in making a process of purification possible. It is a profoundly salvific attitude. It must be continual and lifelong. A religious who professes to live the gospel message in a radical way must therefore adopt this attitude of openness to new experiences, new suspicions, new reformulations of his or her social analysis and practice, new interpretations of revelation and the resultant practice of faith.

This attitude is not one imposed by extrinsic conditions. It is a free option, deriving from an understanding of the gospel message as salvation through the mediation of the other. Thus it presupposes conversion from an attitude of egoism, of "closedness." Here our comments parallel those of St. Ignatius in his rules for spiritual discernment at the personal level. The attitude of openness, demanded by the gospel, is a continuous process of conversion, of purification, as persons continue indefinitely to interrogate themselves and keep themselves alert by means of serious, basic questions deriving from new experiences.

This attitude of openness before the other is a basic requirement of the Christian way of life. It expresses itself as a relationship to the other. It categorically denies the claim of having reached God in some universal mode. Jesus' struggle with the Pharisees began when he identified the locus of the experience of encountering God not in the universality of the law but in the particularity of the other—the publican, the paralytic, the man lying wounded by the wayside, the prostitute, the poor. And the primary sin—unjust exploitation—found expression in the unwillingness to help others threatened with harm, deprivation, and extermination. The modern world, to the extent that it has lost the meaning of the faith as relationship to others, either lives in fear of others or plots their criminal elimination. Life is lived between "fear" and "murder" as expressions of a lack of faith with respect to other persons. "Fear" and "murder" are lived out in a variety of forms, from the crude realism of actual bloodletting to more sophisticated and symbolic forms. And through it all is a constant denial of the other, the refusal to tolerate the other.[11]

In conclusion, we may say that a minimum requirement for a group to exercise discernment vis-à-vis political reality is a critical awareness of the prevailing ideologies, especially the dominant ideology, as well as of the way in which they influence and act upon individuals and groups. A basic attitude of suspicion cannot be lacking; otherwise the whole process of discernment cannot even begin. Suspicion implies an attitude of openness, of refraining from the absolutization of principles that are only relative or restricted in their scope. There are groups of religious who experience a genuine mental paralysis when confronted with any reality that questions their social position. They resort to slogans disseminated by the dominant ideology.

These thoughts bring us to the following problem: If social position is a determining factor in the process of discernment and could have a corruptive influence on it, and we are nonetheless obliged to exercise discernment in the context of a particular social position, then what position shall we choose? The mistake that is often made is to engage in the act of discernment outside the focus of that social position. This is a tactical mistake because discernment can be made only from within that focus. The more substantive mistake is to allow this position to be so swamped with nonevangelical interests that it blocks Christian discernment. What, then, is the evangelical position?

Chapter II

Generosity

Committing Our Best Efforts

If a group of religious is involved in a process of discernment, it is because, at least by implication, they have taken on an attitude of generosity. Otherwise, there is no need to discern, because the choices favoring personal and group interests are made by the simple law of inertia, in favor of the dominant movement. Most of our human actions take place in the context of an economy of mental energies. We do not have unlimited capabilities, and daily life makes innumerable small demands upon us. Of necessity we set up a whole battery of automatic reactions that spare us from decisions that would otherwise drain our energies. This is not the realm of generosity, but that of routine. For if we would try to live in an attitude of intellectual intensity at every moment, we would soon be in a state of exhaustion.

A consumer society with its strident presentation of so many products and goods for sale, all in fierce competition, confronts us with innumerable petty decisions concerning the most insignificant matters. The routine, commonplace act of purchasing a bar of soap or a tube of toothpaste consumes energy, inasmuch as we confront a multiplicity of soaps and toothpastes to choose from, and we spend energy making a choice. Multiply this by all the products and services that compete for our notice in this competitive society of ours! We can experience a kind of "decisional exhaustion." Unconsciously and spontaneously we defend ourselves by establishing habits that will save our energies for the more important decisions.[12]

There is a definite line of qualitative demarcation between the whirlwind of decisions that fill our daily life and those moments in which we seriously commit ourselves to what we regard as fundamental. By generosity we mean precisely that attitude of applying our best energies to those realities, causes, movements, and undertakings that deserve this kind of commitment.

In the sphere of personal discernment, generosity signifies an attitude of anticipation in searching for the will of God for our lives in relation to the matter subject of discernment, so as to commit ourselves to what seems to us to be the plan of God for us. It is safe to say that such a decision calls for a large consignment of our available energies, so that we are not free to commit them to something else. There is an element of risk here in the knowledge that, given the scanty reserve of forces in our possession, the objective we choose could use them up, leaving us nothing for other objectives. God can be infinitely generous in everything. We can be so in only a few areas. And they must be chosen. Here we see a central problem of generosity: Where shall we employ our energies?

Inasmuch as we are beings set upon by a number of immediate needs that must be satisfied, it frequently happens that the field of our generosity, of the commitment of our human energies, will be taken up by these needs. The two basic needs of humankind are material sustenance and relationships with other persons. These could so fill one's horizon and occupy one's energies that life could become a constantly accelerated search for material goods and human encounters, especially when such encounters are pleasurable. An individual's needs end up being the whole meaning of life and, therefore, the field of his or her generosity. Every day we see individuals spending their life blood, "generously" deploying their energies in search of pleasures and material goods to the extent that there is nothing left over for other activities.

The True Field of Generosity

It is much more difficult for us to apply ourselves—expend considerable energy—when the object of our generosity has nothing to do with our immediate needs, those relating to basic necessities, but represents the "gift" of ourselves, our involvement in a cause or project. It is general practice to reserve the term generosity for such a commitment. A person who spends his or her life getting money or pursuing pleasure, even if with considerable vigor and expenditure of energy, does not merit the title of "generous," even though we are aware of how much commitment such activities require. There is a consensus that "generosity" to satisfy one's own needs is located on a descending scale from sheer selfishness down to the elemental instincts of preservation and reproduction. But true generosity belongs to that level of realities that turn outward, in the direction of the other.

Applying these considerations to our study of discernment in the social field, we again perceive this double trend of "generosity" either in the direction of satisfying our own needs or in turning outward toward the other. A "generosity" of the first type corresponds to the commitment to establish oneself in one's own social position within the dominant class and to apply one's energies to decision-making, work, and involvement in that sphere. There are many generous persons—generous within their own social position and in defense of it. They would even be capable of dying for it. Their generosity is comparable to that of those who would work themselves to death to get more money. It is a generosity motivated by egotism, by the instincts of self-defense and self-satisfaction. From the Christian perspective, it is an aberrant generosity.

Christian generosity must move in the other direction. There must be a disposition, a desire, an attitude of making spiritual energies available to work for a change of social position when this is seen as a requirement of the kingdom of God. This attitude obliges us to expend our energies for the achievement of such an end. Generosity does not necessarily mean changing one's position but being disposed to do so, even wanting to do so, and beginning within oneself the journey to that place where the Lord can be followed more perfectly.

The Social Position of the Poor

The Christian must have a sincere concern for the poor, a pronounced inclination toward the less favored and marginalized areas of society, because of the attitude of Christ, who came to proclaim the good news primarily to the poor.[13]

The preference, the option in favor of the poor is unquestionably an evangelical datum so obvious that only a consciousness horribly infected by the dominant ideology could fail to perceive it or could come up with unrealistic ideas and comments as to what it means to be poor, even reaching such absurd conclusions as that the wealthy are really the unfortunate ones and deserve our commiseration.

The poor are not only the privileged with respect to evangelizing activity; they are also the principal carriers of the gospel. Generosity, as a propelling attitude, increases our proximity to the poor. It is only for strongly apostolic motives that we can arrive at discernment of the need to take action among the dominant classes for the benefit of the poor. Whatever incarnates the legitimate aspirations of the poor, the oppressed, and the marginalized will attract and polarize the Christian attitude toward generosity. The center of gravity of Christian discernment is determined by the social position of the poor. It is the privileged, normative locus of discernment—if not physically shared and lived out as one's actual residence and human environment, then at least in viewpoint and interest.

Generosity does not mean neutrality, a torrent of energy expended in the hope that a concrete objective will appear on the horizon of decision. Rather, it means a preference, an attitude of having chosen in advance the social position of the poor. It is only this attitude that can be called generosity. As at the personal level, "generosity," if it is bent on satisfying one's own needs, does not deserve the name, even though it involves an enormous consumption of energy. Similarly, an attitude of readiness, of determination, to apply an abundance of energy in support of the social position of the oppressor does not merit the name of generosity, but that of mere ideology. Generosity is the concrete option to be on the side of the poor. It is only by starting with this option that total discernment is possible in the spirit of the gospel.

A religious community or province that does not have this attitude does not have the prerequisite for discernment. As a result, its apostolic choices will be vitiated in their very root. This explains why some renewal efforts of religious congregations are never more than palliatives and never accomplish anything more than superficial changes: they do not get to the root of the problem.

Privileged Position in the Church and in the Religious Life

The church itself is called "the church of the poor," based on the evangelical logic of preference for the poor. St. Ignatius is quite consistent in his rules for "being in tune with the church"—*Sentire cum Ecclesia*—but it is frequently misunderstood to apply only to dogmatic orthodoxy. It is much more important, however, that this "being in tune with the church" be understood in a way that gives preference to the essential meaning of the church, understood on the basis of the gospel—that is, a community where the poor have a double precedence: both as recipients and as proclaimers of the gospel. Only thus does "being in tune with the church" rise above casuistic artificiality to strike at the roots of the church's understanding of itself. And generosity, as an ecclesial attitude, disposes us toward the privileged of the church. It is only from their social position that an act of discernment can respond to the spirit of these rules for "being in tune with the church."

The religious life is understood in turn only in the context of the church, a place of privilege for the poor. In its various aspects as an experience of God, as discipleship of Jesus, as consecration, fellowship, and a critical presence and involvement in the world, the religious life is understood in its original relationship to the poor. "Embracing the situation of the poor, the religious life occupies that place where God himself prefers to pitch his tent."[14] There is no authentic act of discernment performed by a religious congregation that can overlook this condition for being a religious. And it is precisely because many of them are not made from this standpoint that certain long-standing obstacles are not overcome. The generosity of religious, instead of being confined to an individual level, with no enthusiasm to arouse spiritual fervor, would confront a vast field for the choice and change of position.

Within the context of Latin America, therefore, the attitude of generosity involves a commitment to the position held by the social praxis of liberation. The greater the generosity, the more will risk and renunciation be involved in that position. But in what does this position consist? We can view it at three levels.

At the Level of Interests

The first level involves a choice of the social interests of the poor and oppressed. In a negative sense, this implies separation from and denial of the interests of the dominant classes. In theory this seems quite obvious. But in concrete reality it is quite complicated, because our work in society is frequently tied to the dominant interests, and renouncing those interests would risk the necessity of discontinuing part of our apostolate. And nevertheless this primary level is absolutely essential for discernment.

The question that we must explore in discovering and coming to know our postion better is: What interests are we really serving? We have already seen that we must decide in the interests of the poor. These interests are not necessarily made manifest in some arbitrary definition, but rather in the context of objective conditions. For in many cases the oppressed give voice to interests that have been put into their heads by the dominant class. These have to be analyzed objectively by means that permit discovery of where these interests really lie and what really benefits this or that interest.

The interests of the poor are more clearly delineated when there is a head-on collision with the interests of the dominant classes. There will be moments when we will be uncertain, but there will be others when the difference in interests will have a noonday clarity. Our social position in the praxis of liberation is discovered in just such moments, as we analyze what our choice depends on. In some cases we can be overwhelmed by the difficulty of pinpointing where a real clash of interests is taking place, but this does not mean that we have not taken up a position in favor of the poor. To the extent that we take the position of the liberation praxis and live within it, we shall be acquiring a sensitivity that will permit us to more easily discover the real, objective interests of the oppressed. Our sense of perception, as it relates to liberation, will be educated or dulled depending on whether or not we live on the plane of their interests.

Thus, we are not dealing here with a merely theoretical choice, although at first glance we are accustomed to seeing it this way. It begins with a resolution of the will, with an interior act of decision. Little by little it becomes a part of us through the continual exercise of choices. And its truth is demonstrated in the concrete verification of the decisions that we have been making. The problem for us is that even in the case of voluntary decisions that become consistent, we have considered only the act of decision. Thus we must turn to a second level that has to be involved if the voluntary choice of these interests is to endure.

At the Level of Experience

The second level is to be seen in a search for concrete situations in which to live the social position of the poor, so that we may better understand liberation. Beyond any decision of the will to keep on defending the interests of the poor, we are confronted with the step of seeking to live certain experiences in common with the poor, so as to understand them better and stand more resolutely at their side. We may still continue to live mostly in that social position and milieu where the oppressed are present only by contrast. Meanwhile there is an attempt, at least for intervals of time, to live in the same position as the oppressed, in their concrete materiality, in their indigence, so that the choice in favor of the interests of the poor becomes more concrete, more clarified, and more objective.

Such experiences have consequences, in both the order of knowledge—a closer acquaintance with the problems and interests of the poor—and in the order of emotion—affective commitment. In the first case, it will serve to correct a number of bourgeois misunderstandings and incorrect evaluations of reality. It will lead to a shifting of values toward areas previously unknown and unappreciated. In the second case, the choice in favor of the poor will be confirmed through the concrete experience of living in their shoes. *Fabricando fit faber* (work makes the worker). Our hearts are patterned after our praxis.

It may also happen that the contrast between living close to the poor and then in some other position will bring about an internal conflict within us and require our making a more complete change. We then go to the third level.

At the Level of Incarnation

This third level involves a radical departure from one's social position in order to take up the position of the social praxis of liberation, not just with regard to interests, or even concrete experiences, but by a total commitment. This means a change in one's residence and relationships, such that the position of the poor becomes our normal habitat.

An outright incarnation is entered into within the social and cultural world of the poor. There will always be barriers, especially of culture and language, that will not permit absolute identification. Nevertheless, the tendency will be there. We adopt this maximum possible proximity so that in two lines of development—familiarity and voluntary choice—the interests, values, perceptions, and culture of the oppressed will become our own. Sometimes there will be a slow process of assimilation of the environment of the poor as we seek to be incarnated; sometimes there will be a radical, abrupt transition. At bottom, there will always be some suspicion as to whether persons from middle-or upper-class social strata actually achieve such an incarnation. Nevertheless, it may be affirmed that this choice of living with and like the poor has evangelical validity. Whether identification takes place at a radical or less than radical level is a matter for theoretical discussion. What is important is that such choices are made on behalf of the liberation of the poor.

Another question presents itself: What level of the social praxis of liberation is indispensable in order to adopt a position conducive to spiritual discernment? Above all, there must be a basic attitude of generosity that knows no limits. To the extent that we feel called to an ever greater commitment, to this extent *it* will be a prerequisite to discernment. At any rate, the minimum requirement is an option for the interests of the poor as the social position of our choice.

It will be difficult to continue with our choice if we do not at least seek to live out concrete experiences in a social position close to the poor, where we may perceive with increasing acuteness the problems that liberation will have to tackle. In other words, the basic choice in favor of these interests will receive continual reinforcement as we confront historical concretizations in our own life. This means that the experiences of a liberating praxis shared with the poor will become increasingly important, especially when we feel threatened by the dominant interests that oppose them.[15]

Chapter III

Prayer

Discernment is a function of grace. It is not something that can be gained by effort but is a free gift of God's grace. Thus it is impossible for an act of spiritual discernment to take place outside a climate of faith, hope, and charity. The theological virtues create the necessary spiritual environment. The tradition of the church has persistently emphasized the fundamental importance of prayer in maintaining the theological climate, the native soil, of discernment. Hence the importance of understanding how prayer is related to the three theological virtues that constitute the spiritual climate of discernment.

We are not just studying the tactics for a socio-political operation. We are looking for concrete mediations to bring about the kingdom of God, which is the fruit of God's gift and of our activity, of divine grace and of human decision. Prayer performs an important role here.

Prayer as Clarification of Faith

Faith is above all an adherence, a commitment of one's life, to the person of Jesus Christ, the revealer of the Father. Faith brings us in contact with Christ himself through the mediation of the great tradition of the church that extends from apostolic times to our own era.

Faith is a dimension that encompasses our whole life. It embraces our way of thinking, of forming opinions and desires, of viewing things. It is an atmosphere that both penetrates us and enfolds us. On the other hand, because it is an encompassing reality, it is constantly threatened by distortions. Spurious elements, deriving from collective and individual sin, penetrate this horizon of faith and mingle with it. Thus it may happen that the expressions of our faith take on a number of theologically uncritical elements. We find difficulty in isolating or eliminating them, because their infiltration takes place so subtly, almost imperceptibly. We are bombarded by the communications media and by swarms of suggestions, insinuations, and value judgments often presented to us in a religious guise that obscures their antievangelical character. Our vision of faith is deformed, with a consequent distortion of our Christian interpretation of reality.

And there is more. Faith, as a view of the totality of our existence and a radical commitment, can become attenuated in everyday life. The vision grows dimmer. Commitment grows lax. Here is where prayer is fundamental to faith. It purifies it. It brings our way of seeing the world, human beings, and history more into line with the gospel, purifying it of astigmatic foreign elements. It redimensions commitment. It extends our faith to our lesser acts, so that no recess of our heart and our life is left in the dark. Thus discernment has a greater chance of being clairvoyant. Faith set on fire by prayer puts us in a position to have a more Christian vision of reality, a necessary condition for making a coherent choice on the basis of our faith.

Prayer intensifies the light of faith. It helps us to perceive the religious and salvific meaning of the doctrinal teachings of the church. "Being in tune with the church," which is so basic to discernment, ceases to be juridical dogmaticism so as to be increasingly interiorized, through recovery of the meaning, thanks to prayer, of the various truths of the faith. Prayer permits us to savor within us the truths of the faith. To be sure, these truths of the faith are for many of us a challenge to our intelligence rather than an invitation to live the mystery of God. It is the task of prayer to correct this intellectualism and to show that faith, above all, is life, commitment, experiencing the mystery of God. It also removes the risk of rationalism and "illuminism," which can so easily infiltrate the process of discernment.

Finally, as faith is constantly threatened by these extraneous elements, it finds in prayer an occasion for taking inventory and for purification. Only a faith continually purified by prayer can guarantee us spiritual discernment unthreatened by delusion.

Prayer as Stimulation of Hope

When we interpret a given reality, with the key of faith, we look for a meaning that transcends our own petty perceptions. Faith beckons onward to a universality. Hope enters the picture as that which makes our history concrete, involving us personally in the vision of reality interpreted through faith. Whereas faith speaks to everyone in every age, hope has something to say to us here and now. It is essential to us in that it rescues us from any foreign element that faith might be harboring. Hope brings us into history-in-the-making and informs us that all of this is for us and that our role in it is precisely what faith reveals to us.

In its role of incorporating us into historical reality, hope is transformed into a motivation, a propellant force of history and of our own life. It negates the arrogance of overpowering reason. It works against our tendency to absolutize ourselves and our ambitions. It negates any claim of the present and of the transitory to be definitive. Ideology tends to absolutize a partial view of reality. Hope, as the proclamation of a new future, of an unforeseen and unmanipulable newness, exercises a critical function. In its eschatological aspect, hope is a relativization of human ambitions. If ideology seeks to freeze the historical process in its present structures, hope, with its knowledge of human beings and their potentialities for achievements, proclaims the future of the world and of history as an aspiration to the plenary dominion of nature, the plenary socialization of humankind, in total harmony with the interests of all.[16] It points to a utopia, which has still not taken place in history but which demands realization and undergoes its transformation under the impetus of hope. Hope, in the proper sense of the word, has as its scope the inviolability of a given situation; it trusts in the promises of God and not in the calculated predictions of our human designs.[17]

Hope in particular is the motive power of history, giving meaning to human aspirations for fellowship, justice, and solidarity. From within its genuine eschatological structure of "now" and "not yet," hope affirms the presence of the kingdom of God among us. It affirms the absolute character of God's intervention in history. It affirms the definitive victory of the grace of Christ in the sacraments, in the Word, in the acts of the church, and in the signs of charity. It affirms the final victory of Jesus Christ over death and sin, as manifested in our lives. It affirms that God, in Jesus Christ, has already spoken his decisive, irrevocable Word concerning the world and history. And the effectiveness of that Word fashions history each day in our task of liberation.

Hope sharpens our vision to see the gratuitous nature of God's gift, as opposed to any commercialistic or meritorious view of grace. It negates a capitalistic, accumulative notion of grace. It brings us into the world of liberality, of free, unpretentious relationships with our brothers and sisters.

This spiritual orientation engendered by hope is a must for discernment.

But we are still perverse, tempted to live in quite another way. We are assaulted by innumerable arguments and data that prompt us to skepticism, doubt, and despair. The ascendancy of the rational, the programed, and the structural over the free, the creative, the unforeseen, the original, and the spontaneous is more a source of discouragement than a reason for optimism. Widespread insecurity and fear confront us on all sides. We see the bankruptcy of great visionary dreams. Humanism, slowly and laboriously elaborated by Western civilization, shows signs of necrosis. There are many respected commentators who tell us that we live in a world without much hope, precisely because the scope of properly human outreach is being curtailed.[18]

It is within this historical context of a threat to hope that prayer becomes a twofold necessity. It eliminates those extraneous elements that are rooted in the deceptiveness and arrogance of the human heart. And it activates our perception of those future dimensions that are already present in the mystery of Christ. In a word, prayer kindles hope in us, hope that is sustained by an unobscured discernment in a world threatened by skepticism, fear, and insecurity.

Prayer as Purification of Charity

Spiritual discernment can occur only in charity, love. Charity is quite sufficient of itself. If we were to live charity in all its purity and clairvoyance, we would need neither discernment nor prayer. Our life would be the best of prayers and a sustained act of discernment:

> Love is patient; love is kind and envies no one. Love is never boastful, nor conceited, nor rude; never selfish, nor quick to take offense. Love keeps no score of wrongs; does not gloat over other men's sins, but delights in the truth. There is nothing love cannot face; there is no limit to its faith, its hope, its endurance [1 Cor. 13:4-7].

Our charity, however, inasmuch as it is mediated, is impure. Our love is ambiguous, divided, marked by inconsistencies, infected at the root by sin and inordinate desire. Egotism is endemic. It is like a worm, always present within the fruit, threatening to destroy it altogether. And this is how we are. What guarantees discernment is the purity of our charity. Hence the importance of prayer.

Prayer purifies charity. It kindles the love of God—the purifying force par excellence—in the human heart. It awakens the conscience. It illuminates the turnings and twistings of hypocrisy and sheds light on the darkened labyrinths of our selfishness. It gives us strength to overcome the sin that clings to us. It makes us a part of its own triumph. It sets us free from our closed circle, opening us up to the purifying factor of the presence of the other, especially the architectonic Other, God.

Charity has a missionary dimension. By its acting and being it proclaims a word that calls into question, that unsettles, as opposed to the anonymity that conforms to the given situation. Charity, as a liberating praxis, is the source of discernment. And prayer, in turn, is its life's breath. Charity, in its weakness, gives up easily. Prayer sustains it.

Summary

The prerequisites for discernment relate to an ongoing effort and ascesis. They have nothing to do with static elements, as the term may seem to imply. They are basic attitudes, over which we must maintain a constant vigilance and discipline. Purification, generosity, prayer: three recommendations for our spiritual conduct. And discernment will take place as we so conduct ourselves. As we proceed, there is always something new to overcome.

Here we confront the gospel teaching on vigilance. This is not the same thing as expectation of the imminence of the *parousia*. The scope of a historical evangelical vigilance will lie far beyond this. Today, vigilance is becoming very important in terms of emotional and ideological involvements, kept on edge on such a wide scale by an enormous propaganda machine. Only an attitude of constant spiritual discipline, of an aroused critical consciousness, can preserve our prerequisites for discernment. In this setting, prayer occupies a privileged place as we prolong our moments of reflection in the light of revelation and as we reinforce our voluntary decision on behalf of generous commitment. Prayer encompasses the two preceding elements: it is purification, and it is an incentive for generosity. It also guarantees that we will walk within the context of faith and spirituality, allaying suspicions of excessive politicization.

PART TWO

STRUCTURE OF THE ACT OF DISCERNMENT

The structure of discernment consists in seeking a concrete mediation that will give life to the "general intention" of seeking the will of God in everything, of being faithful to the "Christian universal" of love of God and of all humankind. And this can take place in a variety of ways.

Every act of discernment seeks to perceive how, within a universal intentionality, to put the will of God above all else, so that his will becomes incarnated in the concrete. On the one hand it assumes an interior motive of generosity, unlimited in scope and with no "bargaining" involved, toward God the absolute. In his presence, nothing avails except an attitude of profound readiness. On the other hand, there is an awareness that such an absolute can be lived out only in the details of historical events, always falling short of the universal intentionality.

Chapter IV

The General Intention

The general intention is this: to seek God in everything. This theological, apostolic viewpoint is at the center of Ignatius Loyola's spirituality. His was a revolution in the monastic tradition of the West: until then, prayer had been at the center of the spiritual life. St. Benedict expressed such a viewpoint in his *ora et labora*—pray and work—where the accent falls on the *ora,* whereas the manuel labor, *labora,* is a kind of interruption of community prayer. St. Dominic saw apostolic work as an overflow of prayer and study: *contemplata aliis tradere*—to transmit to others the fruits of contemplation (acquired in prayer and study). Ignatius departs from the trend of spirituality that sees "prayer," especially in community, as the essence of the religious life. He takes as his ideal of contemplation "seeing God in everything," being *contemplativus in actione.* Here is a rich dynamism that gives birth to a completely new view of spirituality, with immense fertility for the subject we are considering here.[19]

We are unquestionably confronted with a new approach to spirituality, where the dynamism of seeking the will of God in everything gives impetus to apostolic activity. This intention is the basis of discernment. Without this, our concrete choices lack an enlightening principle and we are swept away into other sorts of relationships. This quest for the will of God in everything corresponds to the precept of universal charity, where our model is the perfection of God, who causes the sun to rise "on the good and bad alike, and sends the rain on the honest and the dishonest" (Matt. 5:45). Here is a charity that is not limited to our friends, to those who treat us well, but extends to the enemy, to the evildoer, to all humanity. The dynamism of charity is always universal. No one can be excluded in any way from its initial intentionality, prior to the choice of concrete mediations. Thus it is a love without limits, which is not stopped by any barrier of race, religion, ideology, or class.

Discernment calls for a theological atmosphere, which is manifested not just in making a firm decision, not just in doing your best to accomplish what is most authentic, but in seeking the will of God above everything else, such that from this perspective it is possible to decide for a deeper involvement in the history of salvation as a liberating sign.[20] This search for the will of God implies an attitude of basic faith, according to which the construction of historical truth must, for the Christian, coincide with the plan of God, which is a plan of grace, justice, love, and peace. The world, as a cosmic reality and as human history, is seen as a locus of faith, an epiphany of God, a sacramental revelation of God's plan.

The Traditional Schema

We must distinguish between two major schemata that differ in their manner of conceiving the realization of the will of God in the world and, consequently, the way to discover it. The traditional schema, which has something of the Neoplatonic about it, sees the plan of God as pre-existent reality inaccessible to our intelligence. In our work of prayer and purification a knowledge of it is given to us, and we may thus bring it to realization in our lives. The danger is that there may be error in our knowledge and consequently a false realization in our lives. The quest for the will of God is above all a work of investigation, of seeking to know. God's will is pre-existent from all eternity, antedating our human history, and is realized through our actions. This represents an essentialist, substantialist mentality; history is something adventitious, secondary, and transient in relation to the predetermined, transcendent reality. The level of predetermination varies, among adherents of this school of thought, according to their interpretation of other factors, but they hold in common parallelism between history and the will of God, history being the place where the will of God is realized. Faith and prayer will be the major means by which we dispose ourselves to penetrate these secrets of God and to understand his plan, so that we may make it happen. We are the executors in history of an eternal design of God.

This schema stresses the human intellect. It focuses our attention not on history as the locus of realization, but on God, so that we seek to read God's plan in God himself. To turn to God is to allow oneself to be possessed by the vision of faith, as offered by the scriptures and the tradition of the church. In them we find the description of the plan of God, which we are to apply and make concrete in history. History enjoys little importance in seeking the will of God: it is nothing more than the field of action. It is of no significance in discovering God's will. It is not a heuristic factor. It is merely a stage for human activity. The light that is shed on the course of history comes from outside, from the eternal plan of God, which one seeks through the spiritual discipline of discernment.

The Historical Schema

The other schema points to history as the locus of the revelation of the plan of God. We do not picture ourselves confronting an eternal plan of God of which we are ignorant and which we wish to discover, but confronting a history whose theological meaning we wish to perceive. The will of God for our lives is revealed through the theological meaning of history. We are not dealing with a reality apart from history, but with another interpretation of history. For us, seeking the will of God does not mean entering into a relationship with some reality transcendent to history but, illuminated by faith, confronting history itself. Revelation is not the locus where the plan of God is described; it is the key for interpreting the plan of God that is happening in history, which in fact *is* history. This schema presupposes a unified view of history. Human history and salvation history are one and the same thing. At the level of reality, the plan of God is not to be distinguished from human history. Nevertheless, it is possible to interpret this indivisible reality with two different investigative keys. One key of interpretation might perceive only the causality of human actions in the interaction of political, economic, and other interests. But the same reality can be read in the light of revelation, giving it theological meaning, as a way of calling into question our concrete actions. This undertaking is the quest for the will of God. And if we know the structure of human history—and we must know it well in this case—then the "faith-revelation" key of interpretation can open to us the theological meaning of history as a radical questioning of our lives.

This schema for understanding thus requires two basic initiatives. The first is the scientific reading of history to understand its structure. The second will be to read this structure in the light of revelation. In this sense, seeking the will of God in everything will thus imply the need for an attitude of scientific veracity and theological fidelity. One without the other is insufficient. It is of no use to seek the will of God if one neglects a scientific reading of history and is content with an unsophisticated interpretation offered by the dominant ideologies. Where this reading is falsified and ideologized, there is no way that the will of God can be read correctly. The historical schema is therefore profoundly exacting. It will not settle for subjective intentions; it imposes conditions of objectivity.

Faith does not create reality; it only provides meaning. The reality of history lies in front of us in its incomprehensibility, in its absurdity, or in its theological meaning. This meaning is given to us, and we appropriate it, by a faith interpretation. Seeking the will of God is thus a faith-interpretation of a history that has already been read with the analytical instrumentation of the human sciences.

The Frailty of Our Knowledge

These considerations also have to make us aware of the defectibility of our quest for the will of God. We are forever tempted to want to be god-like—that is, to want to know the will of God as God knows it, with that certainty and clarity that is proper only to God. But we are creatures, situated in time and space, subject to all their contingencies. Our access to God passes through a double mediation on our part: mediation in knowing reality—using the apparatus of the social sciences—and the mediation of revelation. In a word, it is by faith that we read another interpretation than what is given us through the sciences. And we find the will of God via the possibility of error in both these interpretations.

Our access to reality is never direct, as it is with God, but always mediated. Our access to revelation, which is itself expressed through human mediation, is also framed in our interpretation, using the theological tools available to us at the moment. Reflection upon this should make us very humble and continually mistrustful of our own interpretations. This is a good antidote to the pride we may feel in supposedly knowing the will of God for us in a clear, definitive way.

The "Gospel Universal"

The drive to seek the will of God is fed by an awareness of the "gospel universal." It finds simple but consistent expression in the "spirit of the beatitudes" (Matt. 5:1-10). There we encounter this gospel universal, this hermeneutical mediation, this criterion for interpreting the data presented to us by reading what the social sciences have to say about reality. Very simply, with the eyes of the spirit of the Sermon on the Mount we can discover what God expects of us, then proceed to analyze reality with the eyes of the social sciences.

What this gospel universal demands of us is an attitude of unlimited openness. It is a theological focus. It helps us perceive that in the manifestation of the will of God there is a preference for the poor, for those who establish messianic justice (the peacemakers), which is certainly not accomplished by an irenic approach that merely smooths over the real conflicts but which is accomplished by those courageous persons who go forward in their promotion of justice to the point of being persecuted. There is a preference for those who put the gift of life above the pursuit of their own interests and pleasures (the pure of heart); for those who are attentive to the needs of the oppressed (the merciful); those who hunger and thirst to see right prevail; those who do not practice the violence of oppression, of exploitation, of lording it over others (the meek), but only the justice of God; those whose life is characterized by the endurance of trials (the afflicted). This gospel universal, translated into the spirit of the beatitudes, can be summed up in the following terms: generosity, justice, liberation, messianic peace, courage in struggle, openness to those who have greater needs, a spirit of poverty.

The Gospel universal is the key of interpretation offered to us through faith in the preaching of Christ, to help us understand that we are to seek the will of God in everything. Faith is the conscience of charity, that which clarifies it and informs it. And faith in turn finds its consistency in reading the evangelical message of the beatitudes.

The Paths of Charity

In the gospel message, read in the light of the current Latin American situation, the aspect of justice leaps to the fore. Charity—love—has to follow the paths of justice.

There are short-range paths of charity where the "charitable" element stands out in all clarity. The parable of the good Samaritan (Luke 10:25-37), the final judgment scene in Matthew (25:31-46), and many other gospel pericopes reflect this viewpoint. A long tradition of humanism within the church has given status to these signs of charity. The general thrust of charity is seen as an attitude of openness to the neighbor in dire need who comes to our notice.

The long-range paths of charity seem to correspond more closely to the attitude that is being called for in our present situation. These are paths that do not lead us immediately and directly to the people, with the result that our efforts do not quite satisfy our sense of charity. We help the people via the mediation of structures upon which our charity is exercised so as to transform them, abolish them, or create them anew, as the case may demand. These longer paths of structural mediations in the field of politics and economics make contact with human relationships where they are determined by laws, political systems, and the like. These changes are a more effective, more universal charity, and thus more "divine."[21]

A Utopian Project

The general intention as a basic element in the structure of the act of discernment is a kind of utopian plan: even if it does not attain realization, there is an attempt to realize it, and this becomes a driving force for mobilization. It becomes like a dream of the future, which, in its function as a motivator of our action in seeking concrete mediations, takes on a critical function with respect to them, denouncing the present order (or disorder) and proclaiming what does not yet exist but which will be the new society. This general intention is a dynamic factor that mobilizes our concrete decisions and thus acts upon history. We are in serious danger when this intention takes on a dogmatic or ideological nature and loses its utopian aspect. Dogmatism and ideology limit one's perspective to special interests, clothing them in robes of universality. They freeze the historical process and the existent structures that they wish to perpetuate.[22]

A utopian plan of this nature necessarily comes upon the problems of justice, as a privileged form of charity in our historical context. It is safe to say that for Latin American Christians, justice as a general intention of all discernment is an imperative of faith and of charity, seen from the perspective of hope. The term "justice" needs some clarification.

The Concept of Justice

A law of language, known to those familiar with classical logic, tells us that the broader the extension of a concept, the less content it has. Extending the amplitude of a term is done at the cost of the precision with which it will be understood. This is what has happened to the term "justice." It has acquired a large number of divergent meanings, some even contradictory, depending on the point of reference. The word has been spread over a wide field of referents and its meaning has accordingly taken on enormous ambiguity.

As a matter of curiosity, it may be observed that the term "justice" is alien to the Marxist vocabulary; for example, it is not to be found at all in J. Guichard's introductory work on Marxism.[23] In the index of the Pléiade edition of the works of Karl Marx the term either has an innocuous meaning or is simply used to refer to juridical relationships that are denounced as ideological fronts.[24] By contrast, in the documents of Vatican II this term appears rather frequently.[25]

We must here define the meaning that we attach to the term "justice," so that our discussion will have the concreteness it needs and not be lost in a fog of ambiguity. In brief, we may distinguish two basic approaches to the modern concept of justice. One is static in nature, the other dynamic.[26] The first of these presupposes a view of the legal world as a given reality to which one must adapt. Thus "justice" will be that virtue by which one is effectively conceded the right to compete in accordance with the rules of the social "game." Society establishes these laws. "Justice" is the enforcement of these laws in relation to the rights that are conceded to individuals.

Paradoxically, the static concept of justice is characteristic both of totalitarian states of the communist type and of authoritarian states whose primary preoccupation is "national security."[27] This characteristic may be defined as "total power," and it confers upon individuals certain rights, provided they are not a threat to its sovereignty. Any act that the state performs in its own defense is "just" and does not entail any injustice against any citizen: it does not violate a right that the citizen possesses. The state itself defines its powers, its limits, its interests, everything that is legal, and therefore all "justice." The horizon of this understanding of justice is closed and static. It leaves a central problem unresolved: How is the "justice" of the law to be determined? If "justice" is the exact application of the law, if it is the guardian of rights that the law grants to citizens, then how can we avoid the arbitrary positivism that we presently experience?

We must turn to a dynamic, critical—we might say "eschatological"—concept of justice. Here the term loses the rigor with which it is defined by the law, but it measures up to its genuine image. Justice is not seen so much as the legal enforcement of decrees, but rather as the evocation of an ideal; legislation seeks to be its historical concretization—limited, fragile, full of imperfections. Justice exercises a critical function: it is meant to judge the law, not simply to cling to it as if to its ultimate point of reference. Justice confronts us with a more fundamental reality than that of the law. It must serve society with an all encompassing view of human relations, derived from the progress that the human race has been making for centuries on the basis of liberative, though painful, experiences. Humankind with its successes and failures is elaborating a concept of itself, of society, that is forever reaching beyond the concretizations that derive from it. The legal world never manages to exhaust this dynamic perceptiveness. Thus, to be bound to a given expression of it is to sell short the reality behind the word "justice."

From a theological standpoint, justice is an imperative of faith and of charity. And that means that in this view of humankind, of society, of relations among persons, revelation has something to teach us. Our concept of justice must start with the twofold experience that is basic to the biblico-Christian tradition: the covenant and the person of Jesus Christ. The notion of justice from this prophetico-Christian point of view loses the juridical exactness of conformity to well-established laws, whether they be distributive (of rewards and punishments), commutative (contractual), or social in nature. It takes on a critical, eschatological, utopian nature. It makes continual reference to the basic experience of the covenant, where God enters into an agreement with the people. Beginning with this alliance, renewed in Christ, we understand that the way we are to live, and our social relationships, must correspond to the plan of God. How are the poor, orphans, and widows to live among the people of the convenant? Can there be an exploited class among the people of the convenant? The very thing that makes the prophets cry out is their awareness of the importance and the consequences of the convenant, which condemns certain laws and customs. In Jesus Christ we are all redeemed, we have all been liberated. We have ceased to be slaves, that we might belong to the family of God. This experience makes us take another look at our concrete reality and ask if the existent "social justice" is a realization of this profound experience or whether, on the contrary, it is a contradiction of it.

Faith and charity confront us with the Judeo-Christian tradition as a source of inspiration to us to live lives of justice. When we become aware that contemporary models of the state subordinate everything to a rigid, hegemonic model of development, and define social justice in terms of this model, it becomes a genuine imperative of faith and of charity to take up a stance of unambiguous criticism, with continual reference to the basic experience of freedom in Christ, of comradely love, of the plan of the Father to establish a people in freedom and fellowship. The concept of justice that is drawn from biblico-Christian inspiration has no plan or strategy of its own, but inspires the choice and construction of concrete implementations. When Jesus opposed the interpretations and customs of the Pharisees by healing on the Sabbath, forgiving adultery, and eating with the poor and sinners, he was

THE GENERAL INTENTION

questioning, on the basis of the experience of the covenant, the Pharisees' concept of justice. He even said that if our justice did not go beyond that of the Pharisees we would not enter the kingdom of heaven (Matt. 5:20). We can say the same: if our "social justice" does not go beyond that of the state, then will not enter the kingdom of heaven.

Paul formulates the problem in terms of a coupling: law and gospel, letter and spirit. The law is a pedagogue that leads us to the spirit and must receive its own instruction from the spirit (Gal. 3:24). Where the spirit exists, there is liberty: we are no longer under the law (Gal. 5:18; 2 Cor. 3:17). Justice, understood from the standpoint of faith and charity, stands in the line of freedom, of a continuing growth of love among human beings. Thus, it is eschatological. Not in the sense that we must wait until the end of time to experience it, but in the sense that we experience it within the dialectic of "now" and "not yet." We are to begin experiencing it in the here and now, so that some day it can be realized in its fullness. Its work is to be realized "now" among us, but with an awareness that the "not yet" reaches its perfected form in a continuous process of overcoming obstacles. The critical, overcoming principle is the experience and reality of God's covenant with the people in Jesus Christ. We must always keep in mind that God is seeking out a *people* for himself and not a grouping of exploited automatons. Prophetic justice follows the path of establishing a "people of God" in the full meaning of that term. It is opposed to the concept of justice in effect in a state where the reality of "the people" is at a secondary level or is not even considered at all.

This work must be performed from within the perspective of hope. And that means: within a context of historical patience, of avoidance of the two extremes of violence and conformity. A violence that cannot tolerate any opposition and wants to eliminate it forcefully and immediately in a quick showdown, without the people being regarded as a people, will never achieve prophetic justice. It is merely substituting one injustice for another. At the origin of all prophetic justice is the covenant of God with the people. Historical impatience does not believe either in God or in the people. It is a revolutionary elite that claims to be carrying out a plan of liberation. At the other extreme is the more common and more comfortable position: being concerned only with the spiritual level and unconcerned with the historical process, as if the plan of God were to be realized outside the historical process. Admitting our insignificance in confrontation with the macrostructures that condition us and oppress us, we capitulate, leaving history to those who believe that humanity by itself can make it and change it.

Hope is based on the promise of God. It is our assurance. It is the promise of a God who is seeking a people for himself. For he has visited his people and liberated them (Luke 1:68). God is concerned with selecting from among the gentiles a people to bear his name (Acts 15:14). We are a holy nation, a people redeemed at great cost; before, we were not a people, but now we are the "people of God" (1 Peter 2:9-10).

This promise of God cannot be either a triviality for us or an impossibility. Hope gives us the assurance that such a realization is possible. Therefore we must take upon ourselves this process of establishing that people through our labors. The presence of God is guaranteed to us until the end of time (Matt. 28:20). All that is lacking is our assent. A position of skepticism, of discouragement, of impotence, of total uselessness in confronting the gravity of the situation is not in line with the perspective of the promise of God, which calls for a kingdom of justice, of love, among human beings. Without *persons,* there is no "people of God."

The general intention with respect to a political option signifies a more concrete adoption of Christian values as the norms for a choice of concrete mediations. These values are expressed in such terms as freedom, participation, solidarity, equality, personal initiative, integrated development, social justice, independence, autonomy, national sovereignty, a guaranteed minimum standard of living for everyone, and so forth.[28] Negatively it involves a categorical, absolute rejection of all violations of human rights, especially the right to physical and moral integrity. This struggle for human rights is another form of charity in the present situation, expressing a general intention in the matter of discernment. This attitude of defending human rights and of criticizing those situations that violate them means nothing more than taking seriously the evangelical message of the beautitudes and translating it into concrete reality.[29]

Summing up, we may say that the general intention—to seek God in everything—is a rejection of any oversimplified approach. It implies an awareness of transcendence, of the utopian, of the infinite, and of the ultimate goal of justice and charity, in an attitude of watchfulness. Its mediations are innumerable, successive, always vulnerable, defectible, and fragile. Were is not for the general intention, there would be a great danger of manipulations, of uncriticized *a priori* assumptions, of special interests, of hidden agenda, of the unconscious absorption of particularistic ideologies.

Of course the general intention is not the same thing as the mediations that stem from it. Without them, it would be ineffective and useless. There can be ideological self-deception in confusing the general intention with a concrete

THE GENERAL INTENTION

mediation. In that case, an impasse can be reached, due to the impossibility of implementing a mediation, which has come to be totally identified with the general intention. And in hopes of achieving a mediation that will never exist, one can end up doing nothing, thus seconding by one's passivity the prevailing situation. Idealism that ends in frustration often comes from confusing the general intention with a mediation that later on proves to be impracticable. It also leads to dogmatism and rigorism in opposition to those who undertake a concrete mediation that fails; they are blamed for its limitations and frailty. Hence the importance, when seeking to pursue the general intention, of concrete reflection on proposed mediations, with the awareness that no one of them can ever be the *only* approach. Confusion between general intention and mediation is always harmful, bringing action to a standstill.

The general intention corresponds to the *non coerceri a maximo*—not allowing oneself to be compelled to the maximum—of the spiritual axiom used to fill out the spiritual profile of Ignatius. And the concrete mediation corresponds to the second part of the axiom, *contineri tamen a minimo*—being content with the minimum. Without the universal, the minimum would be lost in its significance. Without that minimum, the universal would be lost in infinity. The universal critiques the mediation. The mediation makes the universal concrete and incarnates it. It is within the context of this dialectical interaction that the process of discernment takes place. A more detailed discussion of concrete mediation will provide us with an understanding of the other pole of the dialectic.

Chapter V

Concrete Mediation

Mediation as Kenosis

The incarnation of the Word is the *kenosis* of the divine. Instead of going about among us in divine splendor, the Word assumed the form, the mediation, of the slave (Phil. 2:6–8). This abasement, this confinement, this weakness, was the essential conditioning of Jesus' life.

Discernment also has its aspect of *kenosis,* its abasement, its limitations. In its structure it is a window onto the "gospel universal," on the divine content of the universal, and at the same time it must opt for what is concrete, limiting, and human. This is a painful, agonizing dialectic, but indispensable. Without it, there is no incarnation of the universal in time and space. It would be a dialectic that would bypass the gospel. This emerges from the discourses of Jesus, which John has so remarkably synthesized in his chapters on the Last Supper.

On the one hand, Jesus knows that this is the hour for leaving the world and going to the Father, and then his history will take on total, unlimited, pancosmic fullness (the universal). Meanwhile, he loves his own who are in the world, loves them to the end (the particular) (John 13:1). Here is a small, limited, fragile group, whereas Jesus' love extends to infinity. On the one hand, the goal is God, the Father of all; on the other hand, there is no access to God except through the historical Jesus (14:6). The Father's infinite love is found only in those who love and keep the word of Jesus. Only they will live in intimacy with the Trinity. Here is communion that subsists in heeding the word, the commandment, of the Father (14:21-25).

Not being "of the world" goes hand in hand with dwelling in the world. To be "not of the world" signifies a dimension of essence, of limitlessness, of a utopian scheme, of the universal. But we cannot avoid being "in the world," which is a concrete, historical, mediated dimension (John 15:19). Being kept from the world, being preserved from evil, being "of God," are other ways of expressing this same dimension of universality, followed at once by the complementarity of needing to be "in the world," of being sanctified by revelation in the midst of life's concreteness (17:6-19). This dialectic permeates these chapters of John. It reappears in the Johannine epistles. It is important for us to perceive its force. The goal is to be totally of God, to live according to truth, light, and love. None of this can happen except in the context of risk, danger, and decision. The assurance that we will not utterly fail is found in the prayer of Jesus, with the consequent promise of the Paraclete, the Spirit of life and truth (16:5-8).

Politics

We are in history, in the world. This is the place and time for discernment, for search, for risk, for mediations. In this section we shall dwell on the *political* dimension of the options this entails.

The term "politics" is here taken to cover a number of activities whose object is the exercise of power—that is, obtaining or keeping it. In the strictest sense, politics refers to all activity that has as its end, or at any rate its effect, to influence the distribution of power.[30] Politics is directly concerned with the governance of a city, of a state. Political activity par excellence involves political parties, with their programs and platforms, whose final end is to gain power or to keep it. Party activities are those aimed most directly at the world of power and government. They have their own autonomy, and are studied, by the political sciences.

The political sphere reaches out to a series of wider sectors. In this regard the concept of politics is broadened and its relationship to the religious world and faith becomes clearer. To this wider scope of politics belongs the entirety of state involvement, with all its public services; the impact of the political sector on economic, social, cultural, and educational concerns; the political repercussions or implications of economic, cultural, and social activities; the political repercussions or implications of religious and ecclesiastical activities.[31]

We may, accordingly, distinguish three levels at which there are activities not strictly of a party nature but having a political connotation. First of all, there are nonpartisan activities whose political scope is nevertheless quite obvious, for they clearly concern society, such as participation in demands for just wages and in activities in defense of human rights. Then there are other actions that can be regarded as political inasmuch as they affect the political conceptualization of social life (ideology). Here we find criticisms and proposals that reflect one or another conception of human beings and of human relations. Basic to this is a philosophy of human nature and of society. Finally comes the widest level of all, where "the political" is everything that affects social reality, the city, the state, and public life. At this level, nothing and no one involved in public activities can escape the sphere of politics.

There are, therefore, four levels at which the political dimension is understood: (1) party activities, directly oriented to gaining and keeping power; (2) nonpartisan activities with a very direct relationship to the political or which, within a predetermined context, take on a clear-cut political significance—for example, strikes, defense of human rights, defense of the right of assembly, and so forth; (3) an overall philosophy of social life (ideology); (4) the total social reality. At this fourth level, everything is political; every action has its political dimension.[32]

Discernment must take into consideration these various levels of the political dimension. And the influence and normative value of faith varies among them. The problem is always in the concrete choice of a mediation. And, in this sense, politics is basically "the art of the possible"—that is, choosing concrete mediations that appear to be viable at the moment. It is very difficult, if not impossible, to find *one* path that unquestionably circumscribes the borders of the wealth of political directions that may be taken. Politics is "the art of taking aim," searching among the alternatives to find the way to best follow through on the prevailing trends. Working with "the possible" begins with an attitude of objectivity with respect to reality. This requires two types of analysis.

Analysis of Reality

The first step is to analyze the situation in which we live; this is a basic element of discernment in politics. Spiritual discernment at the *personal* level is practically unaware of this necessity. The presupposition is that spontaneous, common sense analysis is sufficient. Latent in this assumption—if carried to the collective level—is the idea that reality is simple, almost transparent, and that by a common effort we may achieve sufficient clarity to make our decision. When our attention is now directed toward a *political* approach to the situation, there is need to face the problem with a scientific analysis of reality.

Epistemological Function

The scientific analysis of reality is made through the agency of the social sciences. These sciences have their own theoretical validation. This means that in general they have a sphere in which they are autonomous and self-regulated, each with its own internal set of procedural principles. They have an "epistemological function" whose regulatory criterion is the scientific validity or heuristic value of their methodology. They are viewed as an abstract totality, self-sufficient and self-regulating at the abstract level.[33] Their scientific analysis of reality, viewed under the aspect of an autonomous sphere, applies to that which they make known to us objectively of the reality in question, and thus make it possible for us to act. Our judgment must be made on the basis of scientific criteria.

Our only interest in the science, within its sphere of autonomy, is epistemological. The human sciences have a "practical epistemological interest—that is, they are intended to increase and widen interaction and communication in society within the perspective of a possible politico-moral praxis."[34] Inasmuch as this deals with an abstract consideration, the ethical value of the praxis to be adapted can be ignored. It is important to know the effectiveness of an instrument, what valid or objective features it has to offer.

At this level the analytical instrument is expected to provide statements on reality, giving us an understanding of recurrent phenomena. It has an internal, logical structure, such as demanded by the exigencies of the subject matter, and says something as to the essence of the reality under consideration.[35]

At this level the analytical instrument has no relationship to faith and is not influenced by political, ideological, or religious pressures acting upon it externally. It is not subservient to any organization that would cause the laws inherent in that science to be replaced by an opinion deriving from the ideological promptings of some outside center of interest. That would be the death of the science. It would cease to be responsive to the purpose for which it exists. It would cease to be a process for formulating models appropriate for interpreting phenomena and for replacing those models with more adequate means of comprehending the complexity of the phenomena, when they become available.[36] Such a criterion cannot be subject to outside pressures, but needs to be judged by some tribunal internal to the science, its own epistemology. The subjective element at this level relates merely to the interest of detecting and uncovering reality. At this level, socio-political interests are out of the picture.

One may speak, then, of a scientific neutrality of the analytical instrument, in the elaboration of a science that has its own internal, self-regulating, self-criticizing principles. The analytical instrument has value in relation to its rigor, its consistency, its orthodoxy, and in its ability to achieve objective findings. It is especially important for specialists in the subject to publicize these issues. Discussions among scientists will help to perfect the scientific value of methodology. In this sense they exercise a function with respect to epistemology.

Social Function

The approach sketched above, although autonomous in its own sphere, needs supplementation. Analytical instruments are elaborated by scientists from within a historical context. That context houses a "social function," which is basically that of promoting social interests. The internal, abstract, and self-sufficient totality of a science does not stand alone in the field of knowledge. It is itself only a part of the totality of existence. There is a sphere within which it is not autonomous. The science exercises an ideological function at the concrete level. It is conditioned by other factors that are not strictly scientific. It fulfills a political function. It operates within the world's geopolitical horizon. It responds to the interests of social classes with subjective motivations. There is need to subject it to ideological and historical analysis to determine its social orientation.[37]

Scientists do not have simply an "epistemological interest" to know reality objectively. Their analytical instrumentation has its origin in a predetermined place. It is not neutral. It is freighted with interests. Confronting a particular social reality as a system of dominant interests, its *place of origin* may be the dominant ideology or some divergent ideology. An analytical instrument deriving from the interests of the dominant ideology will have its scientific prowess oriented in the direction of detecting malfunctions in the system with a view to perfecting that system, and not along the lines of a radical questioning or of an uncovering of the system's contradictions and irreconcilable conflicts. The place of origin has its vision focused in a particular direction and sees other aspects less clearly.

The *purpose* for which an instrument was fashioned thus enters into this same line of interests. We may fashion it with a view to maintaining, reforming, or revolutionizing a system. In all three cases, the scientific character of the instrument must be ensured. For if the instrumentality is incorrect, it will be of no help in maintaining, reforming, or revolutionizing the system. At any rate, this scientific character is oriented toward a goal that will influence the formulation of procedural principles.

As regards our current socio-economic system, we may say that there are two major schools of thought that could have a determining effect on instrumentalities.

The Functionalist Tendency

The basic concern of the functionalist tendency is to define the role that lesser entities will perform within the system. It favors a basic affirmation of society and of the interaction of its institutions. It seeks to know how the life of society is maintained and continued in time, despite a complete turnover of society's members with each new generation. Society interests us because it has certain distinctive traits that are resistant to internal and external variations over a given period of time. Here we find means (structures) by which we may satisfy the necessities (functions) that are the preconditions or results of organized societal life. The conception of society is basic, as we study how specific social elements (subsystems) contribute to its equilibrium.

The understanding of society is dominated by a kind of organic view. An "organismic" method is spoken of. Society, as a living organism, tends to keep its equilibrium. Malfunctions are threats that only need to be corrected; dysfunctional elements must be integrated and adapted to the system. Obviously, the functionalist tendency has a strong bias toward preservation of the system. It experiences difficulties in dealing with conflicts and changes.

For whom or for what the functions of society are performed is not spelled out. The ideological element does not emerge. Rather, it is camouflaged, assumed to be accepted, and unquestioned. Its particular purpose is perfection of the system, the discovery of latent functions, the correction of malfunctions. Its validity lies in revealing the relationships that exist between society, as a total social reality, and the subsystems or lesser entities. Its emphasis is on the form in which an institution will contribute to maintaining the functions of society. Even though, in the hands of English anthropologists, this has been a revolutionary instrumentality in restraining colonial governments from the destruction of indigenous populations, the functionalist tendency represents a conservative position in modern society.[38]

The Dialectical Tendency

This tendency represents a different basic concern. We use this term to refer to the overall view that regards society as a setting for conflict and tension, where opposing interests do battle. Where a functionalist view sees only malfunctions, the dialectic tendency seeks to go back to the basic social structure and see its defects there, at their roots. The conflicts are not isolated incidents; they are the effects of a system based on predetermined relationships of production. These relationships are not healed by a correction of their side effects. There is a radical conflict of interests that has to be overcome, by suppression at the roots. One must observe and study reality in order to unmask it and demythologize the pretenses that conceal its real interests.

The presupposition of this tendency is that one must view society not as an order, an organism, a harmony, or an equilibrium (as the functionalists do), but as a complex, contradictory universe in conflict. It is at this level that the problem must be solved. Analysis of reality must bring us to the point of identifying the forces in conflict, their origin, their operational mechanisms and systems.

Choice of Instrumentality

The subject of our study is discernment. The analytical instrumentalities derived from the two tendencies sketched above are inclined to read reality differently. How shall we choose between them? What criteria will aid us in choosing a mediation?

Anticipating somewhat the section of this book dealing with criteria, we see that we have a twofold problem: scientific and ethical. For the *scientific* problem we have the laws of science. We must choose the instrumentality by which we can most clearly and exactly interpret the given area of reality. Within both tendencies, and between them, there are scientific discussions that aid us in discerning the positive and negative elements of each instrumentality from a scientific standpoint. Each has its advantages and its limitations. One aspect will be worked out more fully by one tendency, another aspect less fully. We may find difficulty, at the scientific level, in making a choice between these two schools of thought.

That we have an option of an *ethical* nature vis-à-vis the overall situation must be upheld. It would be an ideological assumption to relegate the entire question to the scientific level. We would be abdicating our own responsibility if we allowed the choice of instrumentality to be surrendered to specialists in the social sciences.

There is a certain naiveté about religious communities who think they have solved everything once they have invited a sociologist to make a survey of their province and then think that their options are the ones that the sociologist has discovered. The choice must come earlier: Which sociologist (adhering to which tendency) should be chosen? His or her professional competence in the subject is not enough. What is important is to know the ideological assumptions, the school of thought, to which he or she belongs. Our real decision takes place at this level. It would be a vicious circle to have this decision made at the level of scientific competence. There is a time when the circle must be broken by an ethical choice, based on a personal (or group) composite of data, values, and understandings of the faith.

Discernment confronts us with precisely this problem: What position should we take toward the overall system on the basis of our information, values, and religious views? Should it be a general acceptance of the whole picture, in the belief that a softening of the contradictions and a correction of the malfunctions will be enough? There is a philosophical and theological assumption here that the inequalities in human relations (economic, political, and cultural) are not so terribly serious. They should not be stumbling blocks. The basic task is to guarantee the supernatural gifts of faith and grace, which are independent of the enjoyment of earthly possessions.

Without considering the lunacy of denying any connection whatsoever between these two levels of blessings, the fact remains that there is a prevalent notion that the basic task for us is not the suppression of all inequalities. Basically, it is thought that this would be quite impossible. It seems an expression of nature, of creation itself, and so why could it not be an expression of the will of the Creator? There is even a fear that the struggle to suppress social conflicts will generate more conflicts. The best thing to do is to mitigate them. And all this is justified on the basis of "the accepted values of creation." The human universe is taken for a gratuity, the product of free choice and therefore answerable to itself alone. Although it is not directly subject to scientific analysis, it can be probed or verified by a variety of other approaches.

Another interpretation is possible, starting with another composite of data, values, and religious understandings. Inequalities are not an expression of "the will of God" but are the result of an imposition that some individuals and groups have made over others. The uneven distribution of goods does not justify or prove any superiority in their possession and use, but is an indication of service to be rendered to others. The same diversity that characterizes present-day society as an overall structure, where the functionalist school seeks merely to eliminate excesses, is in this other view an expression of an obligation and avenue of service. In this case the choice of instrumentality will hinge on what best aids us in perceiving the contradictions, so as to eliminate them, in the name of the values of the faith. This is a free, gratuitous decision and therefore a responsible one. In both cases there is a risk. Each position makes an effort to illuminate the presuppositions on which its motivation is based. In any event, we are never going to find evidence that will exempt us from making a choice.

Everything leads us to believe that theological reflection in the Latin American context will tend to choose instrumentalities from the dialectical school of thought. It seeks to justify this from an interpretation of faith that sees in the present contradictions the expression of injustice and sin that we must reject. Such a position leads us to choose our instrumentality from within the dialectical school as it is presently constituted, as a means of determining the origin of this situation and, moving on from there, choosing those mediations that seem most conducive to an eradication of the contradictions.

Four Levels of Analysis

This analysis of the situation in which we live relates to four levels: political acts, a series of political acts, ideology, and the system as a whole,[39] which we shall now take up one by one.

Political Acts

First of all, we relate to political acts. Each day we find ourselves compelled to take a clear position with regard to very specific events. Some are clearly political, as with groups that meet for political redress of rights that they feel are compromised; they turn to public protest and other types of pressure tactics. Other events take on a political connotation more indirectly. At present we are observing a series of undertakings in defense of violated human rights.

For some, there is a problem here of the meaning of religious undertakings in this context. Have there been celebrations of the liturgy whose meaning went beyond that of worship and took on definitely political connotations vis-à-vis a given set of circumstances? The problem becomes more serious when either the religious celebration or the refusal to celebrate takes on political overtones, obviously in opposition. It would then be naive to think that prohibiting a celebration of the liturgy at a given moment has the significance of a purely religious act, meant to keep the hands of political forces off the sacred.

This is no way to solve the problem. Discernment here involves deciding what sort of political meaning will be conveyed by the religious act, whether it is carried out or refused. The meaning of a Mass is perverted if it is celebrated to publicize or confirm instances of injustice and exploitation. This would be contrary to the very nature of the celebration, which is a proclamation of the redemption and liberation of humankind by the mysteries of the life of Christ. However, when this celebration has the political significance of contesting injustices, crimes, and violations of human rights, even if other factors are involved as well, it will in no way invalidate the Eucharist. The fact that other political movements in a given situation, prompted by other motives and a different worldview, take on certain features that are actually and objectively in common with the Eucharist, will in no way reflect negatively on the celebration of the Mass.

I limit myself here to the Mass as an illustration, because we frequently find ourselves in just such a situation. When we celebrate a Mass of thanksgiving or atonement, or a requiem, for which the political connotation is obvious, discernment must take the line of searching for consistency between the theological meaning of the Eucharist and the political meaning that has been imparted to the event. If there is such a correlation, there is nothing to hinder the act of celebration. The same holds true for a refusal to celebrate. The refusal has meaning when the social context tells us that the act in question has a meaning opposed to the mystery being celebrated.

In each of these cases it is not enough to establish the objective value of the celebration and its inherent meaning. That is not the issue, but rather its contextual significance. Everything depends on a correct political interpretation of the situation. Without it, no discernment is possible. And the decision to celebrate or not to celebrate will not signal the religious attitude of the celebrant as much as it will his political viewpoint. Inasmuch as the faith contains elements that are critical in this respect, this is what should determine the decision to perform the act of worship or to refuse to do so.

A Series of Political Acts

The choice becomes even more important when we confront an integrated series of political acts in support of a particular policy. These are the individuated policies that in a system full of tensions and contradictions may take on a certain degree of autonomy in relation to the whole context. Thus, it is basic to discernment to get some idea of the relationship between the general ideology and the series of acts under consideration.

There are two levels to be considered. One level has to do with examining the internal correlation of the acts, their meaning as definite, concrete acts. Just taking a simple glance at them can provide us with enough information to take a position, especially if these acts are seen to be hostile to basic values. In many cases just this level of consideration is enough to exclude positive participation. Using means for their own sake has definite moral implications. Although this cursory assessment is not enough for every situation, and we almost always need to relate a particular policy to the whole set of circumstances involved, such a policy may be sufficiently clear and well defined in itself. Thus a segregationist housing policy is something that must be rejected out of hand.

At a second level, the attempt is made to discover the relationship of a particular policy with the whole context, together with an effort for enlightenment to understand it as part of a whole. This may reveal a correlation between the two. Then the result of discernment with respect to the particular policy will be the same as that with respect to the whole context. There can be no compromise with a particular policy that encourages, reinforces, or justifies an unjust general policy in violation of human rights. Thus, to take an example from the educational sector, within the context of an educational policy that is oriented toward keeping an economic distance between classes in order to favor the competitive spirit among students, it does not make any sense to maintain educational projects that are an integral part of this policy and consistent with it.

On the other hand, it may be that a society's general educational policy is ambiguous or even contradictory. It could include laws, standards, and even a dominant philosophy that are unjust and that foster oppression. Here there may be opportunities for a critical line of action within the sphere of educational activity. In this case, adopting such action as a way of calling into question an unjust general policy could be a correct decision growing out of discernment.

There is another, more subtle problem area. Continuing to use the field of education as an example, in the context of a general policy that is incompatible with our understanding of human life and Christianity, does it make sense to inaugurate activities related to a particular policy if there is no opportunity to question the educational policy as a whole? It does make sense if, despite our reservations about the particular policy, our work reflects a strategy of being satisfied for the moment with what little really can be accomplished, while keeping on with hope and preparation for more substantive achievements.

Politics is the world of the possible, not of the ideal. We must sometimes forego the best in order to achieve the little that is really feasible. Our choice here must be that of a strategy for action, not a capitulation. Thus discernment has to be very clear-sighted. Within the context of an overall policy that is incompatible with our Christian views, there must be verification that educational activity we support contains a critical, constructive element.

Ideology

Our level of analysis must go even further. We must seek to become aware of the dominant ideology and its influence on the reality we are living through. We define ideology here as a coherent set of ideas and values that perform the function of regulatory or normative principles for action or political praxis.[40] In a given society there is always a complex of social symbols that take on the form of political, juridical, esthetic, moral, philosophical, and religious concepts. Such a set of concepts that translates the way in which persons understand themselves in various social relationships constitutes ideology properly so called. This is not a scientific, objective, matter-of-fact universe. Nevertheless, it does not exclude truth. What is important is its pragmatic nature, either as an expression or reflection of social reality or as that which justifies, affirms, and reinforces that reality. It is like a cement. It penetrates everything, giving it cohesion.

Encompassed by this ideology, persons see themselves in a coherent world that brings satisfaction. They have a horror of chaos, of nonmeaning, of absurdity. And everything that might seem absurd elicits some sort of response from the ideology. Thus, for example, when we realize that a laborer earns much less than does an intellectual, we are at once given an answer: the intellectual work receives better pay because it is more exhausting, or because it requires more preparation involving long years of study, or because such a person is more competent. For, if necessity demands, an intellectual is capable of doing a laborer's work, but not vice versa. This whole line of reasoning seems very obvious, clear, and convincing. But we do not always realize that it does not necessarily point to "eternal" truth but is oriented to the de facto order established by the dominant system. We may not be aware, for example, that somewhere else a laborer may be better paid, precisely because that kind of work is at the source of the production of values, whereas an intellectual may simply be providing the conditions under which the worker may produce. It is another system, in which evidence and reasoning take a different course.

The force of ideology is, of course, enormous. It also surrounds us with a whole system of attitudes, ways of behaving, customs, habits, and values that seem spontaneous to us and beyond questioning. Actually, this set of attitudes has a very pragmatic function for the system in which we live: it makes it work!

Ideology is a social fact. It expresses the effort of a group to rationalize, to systematize in a coherent fashion its life experiences, its interests, its principles, its objectives, and its conception of human nature.[41] This system of representations (images, myths, ideals, concepts) is endowed with an existence and a historical role within a given society. In contrast to science, its function is to cloak contradictions, to construct on an imaginary plane a relatively coherent worldview that acts as a horizon of experience for its subjects, modeling its representations after real-life relationships and incorporating them into the relationships of a given society.[42] In a word, it is a pragmatic theory aimed at incorporating the members of a given society into its practical life so that the social body will function well. It is important that the social machinery perform well. This means that it is essential that all be convinced that this society exists for their own good and that the better it functions the happier they will be. The pragmatic theory may well incorporate some truths, but its goal is not these truths but the functioning of the system.[43]

This section on ideology has stressed the importance of its analysis for purposes of discernment. It surrounds us, its plausibility and consistency can be questioned only by maintaining an attitude of mistrust and critical awareness. If it is not analyzed, we shall not be able to find correct historical mediations. Political facts or a series of them (a particular policy) are illuminated when seen in the light of the dominant ideology. They will then be seen, in their context, as affirming or questioning the dominant ideology. This perception is possible only when the ideology has been identified and analyzed in terms of its basic elements and most common expressions.

The System as a Whole

The fourth level is the most comprehensive: our socio-political reality as a total system. To comprehend its structure, the values at work within it, its objectives, and the instruments at its disposal, we will need to analyze it.

There are two stages to this. First of all, there is a need to assemble a wide range of information. The Brazilian Conference of Religious (*Conferência dos Religiosos do Brasil,* CRB) chose for the theme of its 1977 general convention "The Reality of Brazil," because it had been discovered that in general there was little information available to our men and women religious on the overall situation in Brazil, whether in the national or the ecclesiastical sphere. Thus there was a paucity of data on which to base options for the presence and activity of religious in the concrete ecclesiastical and pastoral situtation in Brazil. Furthermore, the CRB had noted a considerable disorientation and fragmentation of efforts on the part of not a few religious in the matter of renewal and qualifications for their presence and activity, which was often little more than simply a matter of goodwill and individual initiative, not infrequently in response to immediate needs.[44] This finding of the CRB points out to us the importance of undertaking an analysis of the total context so as to know what consistent, pertinent pastoral options we have. Otherwise, our choices of apostolic mediations could be vitiated at their very roots, with the result that we accomplish exactly the opposite of what we intend. Good intentions alone do not change reality. They become effective only when they are supported by a consistent analysis of the reality they address.

The periodical *Convergência* has offered some very valuable assistance in this area. It has been particularly helpful in the matter of analytical methods, lifting us above the level of improvisation and activism. To get an overall view we have to consider the various dimensions: political, economico-financial, social, historico-cultural. Within each dimension a complex of data is needed. Correct methodology is essential from the outset. One has to know how to gather information. The reliability of the source has to be established, by knowing how to discern the factual content of analyses, criticisms, interpretations, and opinions. Another important question is that of the origin of data: we must try to discover what interests are connected with the medium of our information and interpret it in that light.[45]

The second step is more decisive: interpretation of the data. Again there are two aspects: a critical analysis of the information source and a deep probe of the data collected. The bias of the source has a great bearing on the information itself. The distinction between information and interpretive analysis is academic; in reality, all data are conveyed through channels of interpretation. The mere reporting of an item of information or silence concerning it has significance for interpretation. To make an interpretation we must address each dimension and ask ourselves questions that will help us to understand it. The programs sponsored by the CRB can be of considerable help to us.[46]

In our work of analysis and interpretation we are confronted from the very beginning by alternatives of interpretation. This is a good place to apply what we have said about the two general trends in analyzing reality: the functionalist and the dialectical. Keeping these trends in mind, even if we are not experts in political or economic matters, we can have enough insight to distinguish these trends when studying the analyses of experts. They will have difficulty concealing their dominant interests. And the resonance or dissonance we feel will relate to those interests.

The honesty of social scientists is not to be certified by their having no presuppositions—no epistemological or social interests: this is impossible.[47] But they will apply a number of controls, more or less rigorous, to their viewpoints. Among such principles will be a clear statement of general presuppositions, adherence to an accurate methodology that has stood the test of time, exposure of conclusions to the criticism of other social scientists, abstention from making value judgments when speaking as a sociologist, and a tolerance of those who are intolerant of their findings.[48] Serious, honest analyzers of reality will state the frame of reference within which they are interpreting that reality. To this frame of reference we may apply what we have said concerning epistemological and social positions. It has a sphere of autonomy to the extent that it is submitted to a rigorous methodology and is subjected to the criticisms of those who understand the subject. It has a sphere of dependence insofar as scientists choose it on the basis of the interest that prompt them to make an analysis of reality. There is no such thing as a totally impartial epistemological interest, even at elementary levels of scientific knowledge. Connected with it there is always an interest dictated by the ideology, the view of human nature and society, that social scientists hold.

The more important this task of analyzing reality is for a valid option of some kind, the more the reality will fail to be what it seems to be. This is the first truth to be revealed by sociology, says Peter Berger. Social reality is seen to possess many levels of meaning. The discovery of each new level modifies one's perception of the whole.[49] Generally speaking, our pastoral choices are made on the basis of our awareness of what reality is seen to be.

Political significance is governed by factors other than our wishes and good intentions. And here we are viewing reality as a general system. It is a level that illuminates the three earlier levels and is consequently the determining factor. It is mandatory for us to cultivate a critical approach sufficient to set aside our prejudices and attitudes relating to the levels of ideology, closely related political facts, and more distant factors.

Analysis of Our Personal Circumstances

The interpretive analysis of this fourfold level of reality—isolated political acts, sequences of such acts, ideology, and the overall system—corresponds to one pole of the concrete mediation to be chosen. The other pole is that of analyzing our personal circumstances (or those of our group, class, institution, or profession) in the light of these four levels. Discernment can only be the synthetic result of an interaction of analysis of reality at its various levels and analysis of our concrete circumstances. Inasmuch as we are not dealing here with a utopian project but with a concrete, historical mediation, it must be chosen with an awareness of our de facto alternatives. To be aware of them, we must again make an interpretive analysis.

As regards personal discernment, the will of God is interpreted within a world of the possible, conditioned by what is historical and existential to us. When choosing a political mediation the same criterion is to be applied, with a widening of the base of consideration. Presupposing an analysis of sociopolitical reality, we must then ask ourselves what *we* can do about it. We face decisions where the political element is explicitly expressed, at the level of our awareness. There are three areas of determining factors—related to our personal circumstances—that merit consideration, as follows.

Psycho-Social Circumstances

We must be quite clear as to our potentialities as beings endowed with a psychology and affected by social structures. We already carry with us the freight of our history, both as individuals and as members of a class. Our analysis must help us to avoid two extremes: a deterministic capitulation to our psycho-social history and a desire to ignore it (or unconsciously reject it). Both extremes are fatal. The first leads us to self-indulgence, immobility, and a rationalization of the accommodations we have made. We have creative alternatives. We are not just the result of conditions that completely determine us. It is possible, both as persons and as groups, to be converted.

A certain level of enthusiasm, courage, and cheerfulness is a prerequisite for new undertakings and a departure from old positions.

On the other hand, we have been insisting on the need for analyzing our circumstances in order to avoid irrational enthusiasms, particularly when they are the outgrowth of unconscious and uncontrollable mechanisms, whose consequences are fraught with danger. It seems almost impossible before making any decision, before abandoning a position, to be certain of *all* the mechanisms that motivate us and of *all* our real potentialities. Here we find, then, an application of the "golden rule" of following up experience with periodic review and updating. Our psycho-social circumstances will become clear to the extent that we proceed step by step toward an attitude of revision, of self-criticism and of criticism of each other.

These thoughts apply both to a person and to a group. The methods of Catholic Action, with their threefold program—see, judge, act—are the kind of help needed in such circumstances. Eyes sharpened to see by constant judging are trained to discover the real alternatives for action. And action is in turn reinforced by seeing and by judging. In an interaction among these three factors, persons and groups will meet and recognize the concrete alternatives offered by the reality that is being analyzed. We must never forget that the process is subject to dialectical tension and is illuminated by confrontation with the poles of that tension. There are times when one side or the other will predominate. A certain degree of immobility will provoke a yearning for change. A burst of creative activity and innovations will in turn activate the brake pedal of prudence. Dialectical movement exhibits harmony only in its broad outlines. Over a period of time we may see a person or group moving forward despite the pull of opposing poles, at the cost of suffering, conflict, struggle, argumentation, and high-tension situations. When our eyes focus on the microscopic, all we see is disruption and division .

In the psycho-social dimension it becomes increasingly important for us to be trained in seeing and experiencing conflicts in their midst, rather than to escape to some rose-colored world of pre-established harmony. Our Christian instincts have educated us for the utopia of a new humanity that practices fellowship, the "see how they love one another" of the New Testament, and we feel uneasy in facing conflicts. If we nonetheless struggle for a true solution to a conflict, reaching to its root causes, the positive content of our Christian instincts will have broken through. Usually, however, we attempt

CONCRETE MEDIATION

symbolic solutions, achieving an emotional reconciliation, and the real conflicts continue to exist, in disguise.

Knowing how to live with conflict does not mean conforming to a situation where the battle always goes against the weak, and it is obscured by symbolic attitudes of reconciliation that do not represent any real solution of the problem. Knowing how to live with conflict means continually looking for and choosing mediations that get at the roots. And we must not grow weary of this work, retreating into the alienation of emotional, spiritualistic placebos. We are called to a sustained resistance: the resolution of conflicts at the root level is not accomplished overnight. The contrasts in standards of living are profound, and there are powerful forces at work to hinder the application of far-reaching remedies. Always hovering before us is the temptation to some "third-way" solutions that end up being exposed as conservative.[50]

Our Situation as Christians

It is in the fullness of what it means to be a human person that we come to an analysis of reality. And the Christian faith relates to our existential and historical existence, both as individuals and as groups. Our adherence to the gospel must have some concrete impact on our analysis of our situation. Here we shall not go into the theological criteria for choosing mediations; that will come later in this book. Here we must consider the importance of analyzing this situation of ours as a decisive factor in the choice of mediations. Above all, we need to do away with any spiritualistic view of being a Christian that is reflected in a dichotomy between faith and politics. It brackets out our "being Christian" at the most important moment of the decision-making process—that is, precisely when decisions come face to face with the analysis of reality and we must adopt mediations that are historical and political.

The problem becomes complicated especially when we come face to face with ideological factors whose very intention is to neutralize the critical aspect of religion, that of "being Christian." Despite his clear condemnation of faith in God and of religion, seeing religious faith as an obstacle to the freedom and autonomy of the human person, Karl Marx still perceived the meaning of its protest, its contestation:

> Religious poverty is at the same time an expression of the real poverty and a protest against real poverty. Religion is the sigh of the tormented creature, the soul of a world with no heart, just as it is the spirit of situations devoid of spirit. It is the opium of the people.[51]

Marx's outright condemnation of religion as alienation should sound a resonant note for us, not as a spasm of mental paralysis deriving from anger, but as self-criticism, making religion the "protest against real poverty." Our faith, and the situation of the Christian in the discernment of historical mediations, cannot be used to justify slavery, or as an apologetic for oppression of the proletariat, or to promote the necessity for oppressive and oppressed classes, or simply to make pious exhortations to oppressors to be charitable to the oppressed. We must not make heaven the locus of retribution for all victimization, thus justifying the support of victimization here on earth, nor are we to explain away all the deprivation that victims suffer at the hands of oppressors as a just punishment for original sin or as trials imposed upon the elect according to the wisdom of the Lord, nor should we preach cowardice, self-depreciation, humiliation, servility, humility—in short, the traits of the masses.[52]

Our situation as Christians must make us fully alert to the risks to which our Christian training, theology, and spirituality may be subject because of their inheritance from the past of a collusion with the dominant ideology, and even the service they have performed for it. Christian self-criticism is basic to the process of discernment.

In this area, the theology and spirituality of liberation offer their insights, though not without violent reactions from spheres inside and outside the church. It may be that these reactions, depending on where and from whom they come, may be a sign that we are in fact traveling a true path of self-criticism and we are stepping on some toes. The pain experienced is that of *metanoia* (compunction, repentance, conversion) and of resistance to conversion, so characteristic of persons and groups satisfied with their present status.

Being Christian involves an element of risk, as regards a true choice of mediation. Actually, it is a negation of a false version of Christianity, in the search for Christian affirmation. It takes the form of a process of continually submitting to conversion, to "seeking first the kingdom of God" (Matt. 6:33). To be Christian is to favor whatever pertains to the field of social justice—that is, on the side of the poor and needy. St. Augustine speaks of *pondus meum, amor meus: eo feror, quocumque feror*—that is, my burden is my love; I carry it everywhere I go.[53] This burden of ours, this love, must be a "hunger and thirst to see right prevail" (Matt. 5:6), which finds manifestation today in a solidarity with the destitute and the emarginated. This view of things has to be present as an expression of our situation as Christians.

Our Situation as Religious

There are quite a number of aphorisms relating to the religious life. One of these says that the religious must specialize in the supernatural, that his or her specific function is to witness to religious realities, to the gospel. It remains for the "nonreligious" to become involved in earthly affairs.

This virtually divides the world into sectors, with the sector of the sacred, the spiritual, the evangelical, reserved for the members of religious congregations. This calls for some ground-clearing on the ideological terrain that constitutes the collective conscience of the religious community. This conscience is impregnated with an apolitical mentality and a positive disdain for politics, seen as something alien and subversive to the religious community. By the same token, religious are active with their schools, preaching, youth and adult movements, and the like, in a well-defined political context. We need to examine the "bottom line" of pastoral ministries. The de facto situation of religious should alert us to the falseness of our neutrality.

As long as discussion is restricted to the *political dimensions* of the religious life, not many problems are raised. It is referred to as a sign, a symbol, an eschatological and public witness.[54] The question becomes more complicated as soon as there is talk of *political participation.*

Symptomatic of this problem was the treatment given to a document of the Latin American Confederation of Religious (*Confederación Latinoamericana de Religiosos,* CLAR) on "the religious community and socio-political commitment" that was approved by the thirteenth assembly of the CLAR board of directors, held in Costa Rica, January 27 through February 2, 1974.[55] After a long period of preparation and discussion, the document was never officially published. It was kept as a study paper, due to a number of negative opinions voiced by Latin American episcopal conferences. A major concern of those who opposed its publication was that of the participation of religious in activities—not necessarily partisan—that "would detract from the clarity and freedom of the specific witness of religious." Such participation, the critics argued, would easily be adopted by concrete political forces, thus involving the religious in activities that would be directly political. The paper itself uses very cautious language in this area.

Here is a question that is difficult to treat in a general or abstract way. We are involved here in a profoundly practical field, and opinions are bound to be largely determined by circumstances. But I fail to be convinced by the abstract approach of appealing to the "specific witness of religious" as somehow prohibiting political involvement. Where does one begin to work out a definition of this "specific witness"? Is it to be defined by the conditioning of an apolitical mentality that has no perception of the political implications—even partisan implications—of abstaining from a public act at a given moment? Would not abstention be a political act, with political connotations, when the only way of showing disapproval for an unjust law or an oppressive situation is to perform some political act against it? How could it be objected to that at a given moment, whether we like it or not, the only attitude that calls an unjust situation into question could be understood as alignment with a political or ideological stance?

I find it more consistent to say that the "specific witness" of religious must be a preference for the poor, the oppressed, those without a voice. The witness of religious loses its specificity whenever, by their silence as well as by their pronouncements, they indicate support for the dominant ideology, that of an oppressor. Here even certain *religious* acts will be in opposition to the "specificity" of the religious life. Thus, this "specific witness" cannot be determined apart from reality, but rather through an analysis of reality, with a view to seeing in it signs of support or nonsupport. If there is any specific assumption for religious, it would have to be commitment to the poor as an expression of the vowed consecration to the absolute of following Christ. This means opting for the viewpoint of the poor. Only thus can concrete mediations be adopted. The religious community has no socio-political dimension of its own by which it may confront a given reality. But it resides within a concrete socio-political situation, where it takes up its own position as a critical witness.

The concrete circumstances of Brazil may be described as a situation in which the overwhelming majority live a profoundly dehumanized existence. The religious cannot really understand this except by achieving solidarity with this immense multitude of persons, orienting his or her activities as a liberating factor—but not the *only* liberating factor. The religious is not ordinarily a specialist in economics or politics or organization. His or her specific contribution is not at this level.

The overall liberating process demands that certain values be affirmed, even though they may cause tension with certain liberation movements. By this kind of involvement the religious affirms the dimension of transcendence—essential for all truly human progress—not starting from without but from within. If the "specific witness" of the religious is not *politics,* he or she at least exercises a specific witness *in the context of politics.* This consists in a kind of presence that calls attention to the values of grace, self-donation, wisdom, and control of the rigidity that tends to infect any human project. Politicians have an inner drive to become the "totalizers" of reality and they become identified in an absolute way with their projects. The position of religious does not exclude us from participating in such a project but, preserving the sense of transcendence that goes with our vocation, we must see to it that it be a presence that impels the project beyond its closed boundaries.

Having considered these three conditioning factors—the psycho-social, the Christian, and the religious—and having achieved greater clarity as to the particular reality under analysis, we are now in a position to consider the choice of concrete mediations. Choice presupposes this twofold input, which has further subdivisions. It is a process requiring a persevering discipline of openness. It is all too easy for us to retreat before it, seeking an escape from mediations.

Escape from Mediations

Dogmatic Sectarianism

The most common escape is to lock ourselves up in "dogmatic sectarianism." This attitude has two extremes. One is of the intellectual, methodological order—"dogmatism." It consists in suggesting that our concern should be concentrated in the area of "correct doctrine" (orthodoxy). It begins with the elaboration of universal principles whose canonicity ("dogmaticity") cannot be questioned. They must be based on the letter of scripture and tradition, interpreted by means of rigid canons. The theory is presented in a fully elaborated, "dogmatic" form, and praxis means nothing other than concretizing and applying this theory.

The other extreme relates to "sectarianism." It pertains to the sphere of the will and emotions. Adherence to the dogmatic, as a rigid, unchangeable rule, generates an awareness of ground that cannot be conceded. It is on the lookout to attack collusion with error. Error has no rights. The dogmatic sector confines the sectarian to a tight corner. The dogmatic seal of approval guarantees the correctness and infallibility of principles, so that there is no reason to doubt them. Doubts would be temptations, threats from the enemy camp. It is logical to react against them. The greater the threat, the more sectarian will be the response. It is a world dominated by decisions of the will and emotionalism.

A psychological interpretation would trace these decisions to a number of unconscious elements of self-affirmation and self-assurance. The disequilibrium of sectarian reactions is an indication that unconscious and inconsistent motivations are at work. The rules of such deportment are not those of logic, of rationality, but of unconscious mechanisms. There is a certain outward consistency, but it has no relationship to the rules of reason. It obeys the laws of the interactions of the individual's implanted impulses.

Why is this attitude of dogmatic sectarianism an outright escape from mediation? Perhaps it would be more accurate to say that it is a flight from the choice of mediations. It is blind to the fact that the elaboration of dogma does not take place in a vacuum. Dogma is not simply "given," and then translated into praxis. Dogma is first discovered in a praxis; it seeks concretization by determinate mediations. Opting for sectarian orthodoxy means that one has already chosen in advance a certain sector of mediations before the work of discernment could begin. Choice has been circumvented, preempted. This is an antidialectical attitude in the marrow of a dialectical reality.

Not knowing that there is a dialectical relationship between theory (dogma) and practice (concrete mediation) does not mean that it does not exist. Dogmatism is unaware of the factors determining its position, which in turn will condition its choices. From within a sectarian attitude, there is no room to criticize and question, and predetermined choices are immune to reformation. And this means withdrawing definitively from the process of choosing mediations.

Furthermore, at the root of such an attitude is an emotional, voluntaristic substratum that resists all reasonable argumentation. It has to do with another kind of reasoning. From such a position it is difficult to create the conditions for discerning concrete mediations. At best, they will be restricted to a well-defined, predetermined handful. And anything that is not within the bounds of sectarian orthodoxy will be automatically excluded *a limine*.

Universal Neutrality

Another refuge is "universal neutrality." This position constitutes the opposite extreme. In dogmatic sectarianism persons settle into a restricted area and make choices only from that context. This disallows the privilege of questioning. The other extreme is taken up by those who want to be so open as to make "neutral universalism" their ideal. No limitation whatsoever is accepted as contrary to the universal charity demanded by the gospel.

This is the classic confusion of a utopian objective with a concrete mediation. Universalism applies to the objective; mediation has to be kept within limits. And there is no such thing as neutrality. For the Christian objective to have a universal dimension it has to embrace friends and enemies, Jews and gentiles, blacks and whites, oppressors and oppressed, Christians and non-Christians, the civilized and the uncivilized. The objective seeks the resolution of any and all contradictions. It is the motivating principle of concrete processes that take place only and through limited, historical mediations.

"Universal neutrality" means in practice that one chooses mediations without correctly perceiving their *partial* character. This involves a great risk because one loses the possibility of exercising control. Control presupposes a keen awareness of reality. And to choose on the basis of a partial perception of values, thinking it to be included in a neutral universalism, inhibits a critical, questioning attitude. The possibility of accepting criticism is lost; there is no way of knowing that one chooses on the basis of a limited reality and that the choice could be called into question by other aspects of the same reality. "Neutral universality" hovers above all these partial questionings and remains untouched by them.

Furthermore, for the Christian there is no such thing as an unlimited pluralism or a neutral universality. For there is revelation. There is the person of Jesus Christ who, in his historicity, is the pattern for our own lives. Not everything can be included in the vision of the kingdom of God. The kingdom demands that choices be made. It leads ineluctably to partiality. It specifies which direction our decisions must take. "No Christian has the right, without betraying the faith, to adopt decisions that accept, create, or consolidate what revelation or the human conscience rebukes."[56] All mediations must relate to the universal intention of the gospel. All pluralisms must respect the limits imposed by gospel inspiration.

There is a certain kind of liberalism that does not seem compatible with the Christian view. It is formulated in terms of an unlimited pluralism: the freedom to choose any mediation whatsoever, provided it respects the privacy of the individual. The presuppositions of such a position are highly questionable. It presupposes the autonomy of the individual as an integral reality in itself, on which its understanding of society is based. It overlooks the dialectical relationship between the individual and society. Furthermore, it pays exaggerated tribute to a central category of modern thinking: the triumph of reason over nature. This is a profoundly individualistic reason.[57] This kind of liberalism provides legitimacy, confirmation, and impetus to an extremely oppressive system. It is an ideology that favors an economic system based on the private, exclusive ownership of goods, unlimited in dimension and devoid of responsibility or social commitment.

When such an ideology permeates us, we easily fail to perceive the errors of a supposedly open position of tolerance for any mediation whatsoever. Such a position is of interest to those who are impatient of criticism and have something to lose if changes are made. Liberalism justifies its own postion. Those whom it favors want to keep it in effect. When liberalism is applied to the economic sphere it leads to a number of contradictions, including an enormous disparity between classes, making of political liberalism a two-edged sword. Opposition can build up to such an extent that it becomes threatening to the economically well-to-do classes. What happens then is that a political authoritarianism is imposed alongside economic liberalism, so that it will be possible, by repression, to maintain a situation where even the most flagrant contradictions are suffered in silence. Even where liberalism is defended as an ideology that justifies a situation of privilege, in practice it has gone far beyond this role.

Another questionable presupposition is the limitless value assigned to the individual. Personal freedom becomes practically godlike. By the same token, in practice a profoundly oppressive society is being created, in which persons end up destroying themselves. If atheistic criticisms of the eighteenth and nineteenth centuries attacked the transcendence of God as a force that oppressed and debilitated human beings, in the twentieth century we have seen economic transcendence take control of them and glorify one segment of humankind while oppressing the great majority. Here is a concrete realization of the *homo homini lupus* of Thomas Hobbes—the human person preying like a wolf on its own kind.

Both the "sectarian partiality of dogmatism" and "neutral universalism," which unquestionably makes a pretense of neutrality, shun any genuine discernment of concrete mediations. Such mediations call for commitment.

Mediations and Their Exigencies

Mediations have to be adopted in the concrete and with commitment. We live in a real, factual world. The only truth is that which can be verified (*verum + facere* = to make true). The adoption of mediations presupposes on our part an effective commitment of ourselves, in the development of a project, a cause, or a movement.[58]

What are these requirements? Negatively, we may say that they exclude any sort of indifferentism, superficial irenicism, or political relativism. These are attitudes resembling the "neutral universalism" discussed above.

Ignatian indifference has nothing whatsoever to do with a lack of commitment. It has an acute sense of transcendence that penetrates critically to the very interior of mediations, unveiling any elements of relativity or caducity, even though they may be unavoidable in the concrete. It is a sword that cuts deep to expose the inner core of reality, its reference to the Creator.[59] Ignatian indifference is aware of the fact that our way will become vague and indefinite if transcendence does not imbue a concrete mediation. A tension exists between the transcendental and a "here and now" that could be different.

Indifferentism as a noncommittal attitude is cowardice, fear, a sin of omission, a failure to face risk. It could also reveal an unwillingness to face up to our creatureliness and historicity, our desire to experience total fulfillment *now*. It yields to the temptation of Genesis: "You will be like gods" (Gen. 3:5). It is a quest for the peace of stagnation, the fruit of neglect, rather than that of overcoming life's conflicts. This is a pseudo irenicism, not real peace. Peace does not come from outside us, or from omissions, or from ignorance of tensions, but from the option for concrete mediations in line with a utopian objective. This can take its birth only in freedom, which implies profound structural modifications, reaching even to the economic anatomy of a society.

Again in a negative way, discernment of concrete mediations cannot be of the cookbook variety. The need to be concrete does not mean descending to the level of casuistry, where innumerable "test cases" have been thought out and resolved. Unfortunately, some literature on violence reflects this abstract, casuistic approach. Although because of its minutely detailed nature it seems to be a profoundly concrete approach, closely related to real life, it is in fact a warehouse of abstract, disincarnate thinking. This is because casuistry is based on abstract universal principles, quite tenuously related to the facts. Its flair for descriptive details derives from the imagination, not from history. Furthermore, it is located within a certain sphere of interests—without being aware of it—and from within that sphere it pontificates on *all* situations.

In reality, it is only from within a concrete process and commitment that a choice is possible. There is a hermeneutic circle in action here. We give an interpretation to a situation, while being interpreted by it. We view a reality and at the same time this reality provides us with the lens we use to see it. Casuistry refuses to recognize this dialectical interplay. It confines itself to its inherited hermeneutic universe. The Copernican revolution has not taken place on this terrain.[60]

The exigencies of concrete mediation have a *positive* side as well. First of all, they must retain their dialectical nature with respect to the gospel universal. As specific mediations they must never be viewed and evaluated for their own sake, apart from their relationship with the utopian universal of which they are concrete expressions. The basic requirement of any concrete commitment deriving from discernment is this: to constantly confront the "general intention," never ceasing to activate, purify, make corrections, and take new steps in light of it.

When adopting concrete mediations we find ourselves in a situation where it may be necessary to renounce certain values of the gospel in favor of others judged more important at the moment. We face here a difficult strategical problem in which some values are sacrificed in the light of a long-range goal of wider scope. Because politics is the art of the possible, we find ourselves subject at any given moment to this expedient of choosing what is more opportune. We are here on the verge of a completely justified "opportunism." We have the task of adopting a structure as a concrete mediation, with the awareness that in doing so we are renouncing certain well-defined values in the hope of gaining others.

Mediations within Religious Congregations

For many younger persons, entering a religious congregation means adopting this perspective. A religious formation unrelated to the general population, taking place under bourgeois circumstances, with an abundance of resources available only to the rich, seems to have no meaning at this moment of history. This could not be the orbit of freedom. On the contrary, it seems more like the orbit of oppression. Training received in this context will only with difficulty lend itself to some other situation, where one could be of service to those who are really poor. It seems quite remote from the utopian objective. Only if there are seeds of hope for a realization of that objective can the choice of this mediation find acceptance.

The utopian objective and the general intention of service to God and commitment to the Absolute in concrete service to the needy, which is more and more beginning to be the motivation behind vocations to the religious life on the part of young persons, confronts the concrete mediation of an institution, sometimes centuries old, encumbered with structures having little orientation toward this general intention. The judgment that a mediation fails to correspond to certain values for a given period of time, but will do so over the long run, may be realistic. Nevertheless, vigilance must be maintained, to avoid falling into an accommodating opportunism and ending up abandoning the utopian objective, turning instead to mediations that are in no way a concrete expression of it.

CONCRETE MEDIATION								71

The greater the lack of evangelical inspiration in one's orientation to these choices, the more difficult they will be. We must take into consideration a variety of factors: psychological, educational, ideological, all dependent on one's knowledge of other areas. Mediations are not chosen in a perfect purity of intention but in an interaction of human emotions, with a mixture of selfish interests, subject to a chance combination of circumstances. Thus, when we study the existence of certain concrete mediations in the religious life of a congregation, we must apply a series of tests along these lines. The very imperfection of present structures is often due to the limitations of certain persons who in a given situation exercise the power of decision and may initiate a sequence of events that will bend a community in an inappropriate direction. And an initiative of this kind, which results at any given moment simply from the opinion of one or a few persons, then becomes a burden that is hard to remove.

The mediations with which we are confronted in the political sphere must be discerned on the basis of the concrete judgments on persons and situations that give them meaning. Any elements of an ideological nature, related to our sociological, political, or scientific awareness, will interfere with the discernment process. These factors will have only an indirect relationship to faith. Faith performs more of a selective than a creative function with respect to these factors. Considered in their autonomy, these factors have their own heuristic norms. Faith serves us more as an indicator of blind alleys, restraining us from certain alternatives because they are incompatible with revelation. Meanwhile the area that is left open to risk, to freedom, to choice, on the basis of our awareness of some other sector than that of revelation, is enormous. This is the "frequency band" on which pluralism operates.

In practice we will often have to work out a hierarchy of values corresponding to our concrete situation, as the basis for making our choices. This hierarchy will be profoundly influenced by historical and circumstantial factors. This is not an abstract ordering of values; it is concrete. It has to do with an order of feasibility—that is, the possibility of achieving the values in question. A less important mediation, with little meaning for the population as a whole, may at some given historical, circumstantial moment become the first choice, inasmuch as the most important choice of all is still outside the realm of possibility. In other words, in order to successfully adopt a more important mediation, it will often be necessary to create a series of conditions that make it possible. And these conditions may turn out to be mediations of a lower order of desirability. Nevertheless, they are possible at the moment. Impatience in dealing with the exigencies of certain mediations has delayed many a process. All genuine change has its preconditions. When they do not yet exist, the undertaking in question has to include their creation.

Once again applying these thoughts to the religious life, we see that there are many who wish their congregations would live a life closer to the poor, whereas the majority, in fact almost all religious houses and apostolic works, are quite remote from the masses and relate rather to the more well-to-do classes. In view of this situation, so acute for many religious, one can agree to the importance of choosing less drastic mediations while still proceeding slowly toward the possibility of adopting stronger mediations. This is not an easy path to follow. Nor does it necessarily cancel out an approach advocating "shock therapy." In medical practice the patient usually gets well quickly or else undergoes irreversible brain damage. At the social level, a similar thing can happen. It is possible for a group to make rapid, sweeping changes by the choice of more drastic, violent mediations. But there is also an enormous risk here of incurable schisms within the group, and of dangerous radicalizations. It demands exhaustive analysis of a group's possibilities. Analysis, however, would obviously never spare us the risk of error and would never substitute for the courage that would be needed to embark on such a venture.

Unity or Pluralism?

Inasmuch as the discernment of mediations presupposes the conjunction of several elements, some oriented toward an understanding of revelation (faith), others toward socio-analytical probings of reality, the field of possibilities may be extensive. Meanwhile, there is nothing to prevent a group of Christians, a religious community, or even a whole province, from arriving at a collective consensus on highly concrete mediations directed toward a well-defined political goal. This is a practical, concrete, rather than an abstract, consensus; unanimity derives from a precise interplay of circumstances.

The question is whether to seek such a consensus or to deliberately cultivate pluralism. Both positions run the risk of becoming reactionary. The concrete choice of a single mediation might easily degenerate into authoritarianism and dogmatism, leading to an oppressive situation. But no one can deny that its effectiveness on certain occasions is much greater and it could even be demanded because of the seriousness of a particular set of circumstances. Pluralism could also lead to a reactionary position to the extent that it attenuates a more concentrated criticism. We are assuming that this involves an area where there is an alliance of powers of such a nature that the

CONCRETE MEDIATION 73

calling of one of them into question means dealing with all of them. We also assume that one of these powers has gone to the very limits of arbitrary decision. To challenge this arbitrariness may be seen as the only possible Christian stance, even though it has wider implications in the concrete. It would be reactionary to call for a pluralism of possible attitudes, because this would attenuate the critical force of the confrontation.

Such a hypothetical example, described in such vague terms, simply demonstrates the lack of contradiction between "the obligatory singleness of a concrete mediation" for a group and the theoretical, abstract alternative of pluralism in a field where there is a conjunction of various elements deriving from such distinct sources as revelation and socio-analytical findings. Discernment is to be a process that makes possible the existence of such a situation, because it always takes place in the concrete and must seek to adopt the best mediation for a given set of circumstances.

Summary

We are attempting to see the structure of the act of discernment as a quest for historical and political mediations of a concrete nature, where there is an incarnation of the "Christian universal," the utopian objectivization of the kingdom of God, the will of God. We see this as a complex process. These two factors must be understood in a dialectical rather than a sequential way. This means that one need not plan a utopian realization of the kingdom in advance or describe what is the will of God and then in light of this seek out the mediations. No. The will of God and the kingdom of God are illuminated by a dialectical interplay of mediations. The general intention sheds light on the mediation, and this in turn explains, illumines, and concretizes the general intention.

We see the will of God, searched for fundamentally in discernment, as a reading of concrete history by faith, and therefore in the light of revelation. This concrete finding then calls into question our reading of faith, raising new questions, arousing new suspicions, to which only a new hermeneutic of faith may respond. There is no place here for an easygoing attitude that seeks to find new answers framed in old language, with just a slight coloring of the modern.

The world of mediations is history. From within history, apparently made up of a set of fortuitous events deriving from an inextricable network of factors working together, the process of discernment seeks to detect the underlying thread of the plan of salvation and to make choices in its light. A discovery of this type does not depend just on a knowledge of the faith. It is a second reading that presupposes the best possible exposition of socioanalytical structures, the unraveling of the tangle of happenings that will yield to analysis by a number of instrumentalities furnished by the human sciences. This locates us in the universe of pluralist culture where we have to make choices. I have attempted to throw some light on the relationship between these two factors.

I have sought to assist the reader's comprehension of the complexity involved in the spiritual exercise of discernment, especially as it relates more directly to the political field. Until now, this has been a sphere rarely visited by theologians of spirituality, and simply abandoned to other professionals. A more encompassing vision of faith, with special attention to epistemological autonomies, has led us to perceive its role in such a process. There is not an existential independence here, but merely an abstract, formal distinction between the epistemological universe of socio-political analyses of reality and the social position delineated by options of an ethico-religious nature. It is the relationship between these two positions that enables and requires us to exercise vigilance in discernment. There are various ways of realizing this process in our personal or group life. Ignatius considered these methods at the *personal* level, referring to them as moments of choice. We shall attempt to reinterpret them within the context of our own field of vision—that is, with reference to *politics*.

CHAPTER VI

Types of Discernment

The various ways of conducting discernment may vary according to the groups or individuals involved, and even for the same individuals and groups, depending on diverse occasions and situations. Following the lead of Ignatius we shall attempt to reduce these procedures to three types, using as our criterion the variety of reactions instigated by the action of God. This means that we will be interpreting three different psycho-social situations, three ways in which God acts, relying upon the scriptures and church tradition for interpretation.

We shall not linger over the psycho-sociological interpretation of the structures involved; we shall apply a theological hermeneutic. In doing this we do not disparage or reject any other types of interpretation. These interpretations can be elaborated and will illuminate reality from another angle. No one interpretation is exhaustive. The interpretation of faith is just that: an interpretation. It does not coincide with total reality. It is interpretation aided by the key of revelation, which is something given to us and which we accept by faith.

The Intuition of the Mystic and the Prophet

This is the fast route, the shortcut. At times it becomes the dialectical synthesis between the "general intention" and the "concrete mediation." Instead of traveling the long route of analysis, the mystic and the prophet provide an instant testimony. Of what does this consist?

There are two factors at work: the concrete situation with its possible mediations and the concrete status of the individual or group. The mystic or prophet, who can be either an individual or a group, has a clear insight of the situation, in the light given by God, as an expression of justice or injustice. Such a person or group sees everything as black and white, not concerned with the grays. It is a general judgment, usually radical, with a clarity that would be reckless if it were not perceived as a witness to the light of God. At the same time it perceives just what attitude to adopt to bring everything into play. The psycho-social, the Christian, and possibly the religious situation are seen as a simple unity.

In our context this type of discernment is sometimes revealed in the radical option of solidarity with the poor, with such clearness that the individual or group is led to radically renounce the privileged position with which they have been identified. With prophetic confidence, they seek to live with the poor.

Characteristics of such a discernment are the clarity, the inner certainty, and composure regarding the option revealed by intuition, even though many opposing reasons are presented and even though no rational, logical response can be given to them. The mystic or the prophet does not allow entrapment by any sophisticated arguments on the part of opponents or interrogators. His or her certainty is not shaken, whether by threats or by any chaos that may have erupted, from the firmness and originality of the decision that has been made. In general, these are decisions that entail a rupture of deep, emotional bonds. There is a painful gap that would be difficult to bridge without this interior clarity.

When such an intuition comes into collision with the institution, with "obedience," then we have the classic case of "conscientious objection." For the demands of God are perceived, in conscience, with such clarity that a *no* would be understood as a betrayal of the Absolute. At this level, there is no human authority that can stand in its way.

The more radical and original the decision, the greater the certainty and clearness must be. For the risk of self-delusion, of arrogance, of obstinacy, of the psychological projection of problems, is always present. Decisions can be tested by certain criteria, if not at the moment when they are made, at least after viewing the consequences. The individual or the group must take into consideration factors that would shield them from self-delusion. We must not allow the entire process to take place at a purely subjective level. A critical judgment will be based on factors studied in Part Three of this work, "Criteria for Discernment."

Perhaps the example of Francis of Assisi and his early followers will help us to understand this kind of choice. He did not have in mind to found a religious order. He clearly sensed the need of assembling a *novus populus* (a new people) who would follow the Sermon on the Mount in all purity, obeying the gospel *sine glossa* (unvarnished) and using it as its direct "rule." To follow the teaching and example of our Lord Jesus Christ—that was all he wanted.

Francis resisted the idea to have his "new people" recognized as a canonical religious order. His "new people" was the antithesis of the monasticism of that time. It had lost its original identification with the landless and the poor. Its missionary ardor had cooled. The *fuga mundi* (flight from the world), the *peregrinatio evangelii* (pilgrimage of the gospel), and the original internal dynamism had lost their force in contemporary monasticism. Francis said *no* to this institution, which had compromised itself with the socio-political structures around it, lending support to the feudal barons. The faith had lost its original vitality in society. Francis wanted the "pure gospel," devoid of theological interpretations and commentaries, a fellowship of the poor with the poor. It was a witness that came to him from the intuition of a mystic and a prophet. His was a daring, revolutionary enterprise, whose success could be perceived only from some later vantage point. He said *no* to the existing, concrete forms of contemporary Christianity. His was a radical, prophetic protest. His *no* to the de facto forms of Christianity did not prevent him from maintaining his *yes* to the church.[61]

Neither the evidence presented by the institutions nor his own insignificance and unpreparedness in spiritual things could make Francis doubt the clarity with which the call of God had come to him. It is easy for us to say this today. Francis has been canonized. The Franciscans are alive and well. But at the turn of the thirteenth century it was not so simple to detect the total significance of this process. Francis, by what he did, had moved very close to condemned heretics, whose work had been lost to the life of the church. Nevertheless, he had to take the risk of walking in the light of his decision, together with those who had joined him in inaugurating the Franciscan experience.

We may say the same of contemporary groups that have been trying out new, risky experiences. To the extent that they clearly perceive the call of the kingdom of God, they will have to make this attempt. The clearness of insight of the mystic and of the prophet does not absolve them from responsibility. They are not above the necessity for decision. They will not be spared the internal pain that comes with making a break. Certainty and firmness based on the grace of God will be present in every true charismatic movement. Those who are on the sidelines of experience will always regard it with suspicion. It is to be hoped that they too will come to approve and promote such experimentation.

The Doubt and Anxiety of "Existentialists"

The clarity of the mystic and the prophet is not very common. Most of us live in the to and fro of an oscillation, a swinging of the pendulum between clarity and confusion. There are moments when everything seems easy and clear and already decided. There are other moments when everything seems dark and difficult and impossible. On the one hand, there is a hesitation to leave one's own "position" in a radical way, while on the other there is apprehension about continuing in it out of cowardice. We are attracted first by change, then by permanence. Plausible reasons present themselves on both sides, our spirit is elated and saddened, first in one direction, then the other.

The anxiety that one will capitulate to the desire to stay put, without taking the risk of a proposed innovation, is combined with the fear of being quixotic that goes with taking a radical position. After all, there are many holy persons, with more virtue than I have, who do not make the change that I think is needed, who do not opt for assuming this new position. This is an anxiety that attacks many in a religious community when they want to live closer to the poor and oppressed. They look around them and see how generations of religious—devoted and edifying persons—continue to this very moment in their bourgeois social positions. So then, would it not be extremist to insist on the need of changing one's position as an expression of fidelity to the gospel and to the prophetic impetus of the religious life?

This swing of the pendulum inflicts pain by the lack of clarity and the insecurity it brings with it. At times it seems that only an individual or communal life that is devoted to the process of liberation finds completely meaningful fulfillment for the Christian and the member of a religious order. It really does not matter that others do not do it this way or see it this way. One is responsible for one's own conscience. And the political level at which a person is trapped can vary widely and will be independent of religious values. Here anxiety disappears as one turns to the light.

The pendulum sometimes swings toward joy and peace, sometimes toward doubt, uncertainty, and the consideration of alternatives. This applies not only to some great conversion and change of position but also to the choice of other, less momentous, concrete mediations.

Symptomatic of our era is the perplexity experienced in reading the life of Jesus, the scriptures in general, and church tradition. For each alternative involved in a decision, there seem to be corroborative examples in the gospel. There is a danger of forfeiting the totality of Christ's message by preoccupation with all the pros and cons of a decision. The reading of the gospel can be profoundly conditioned by these various swings of the pendulum of indecision. The *yes* of a mediation reads the texts of scripture, seeking confirmation. The *no,* on the other hand, also assembles its collection of confirmatory texts. And whenever discernment is made in a group context, scriptural texts crisscross in the twilight zone between alternative hermeneutics.

Two Exigetical Equations

The impasse is primarily the result of a false understanding of biblical interpretation. There is a traditional schema that promotes this type of textual interplay. We set up two interrelated factors: the life of Jesus and the life of the Christian; Jesus' situation and the situation of the contemporary Christian. Beginning with this two-member equation, we look for parallels between Jesus and the Christian, between Jesus' situation and that of the Christian. Where factors correspond, they are seen as normative. An example may help to make this clear. Jesus lived in the midst of a usurping empire, that of the Romans. He experienced the temptation of the Zealots, who were trying to draw him into their cause of liberation by means of armed force. The Zealots seem to have had some affinity with many of Jesus' teachings, and they felt that they could count on him in their military uprising against the Romans. Jesus had no interest in this, which caused a crisis for many of them. This may have been the reason why Judas became disillusioned with Jesus.[62] We too are living in a society dominated by usurpers. There are groups that want to instigate a social revolution, even if this means violence.

Here we have the terms of the equation. The conclusion is that, just as Jesus did not assume a political stance on the situation of the usurper, so also we Christians, as Christians, should not adopt a stance on our situation of being dominated. As may be seen, this type of exegesis is based on an isotropic relationship that equates the situation of Jesus with our own. This is absolutely wrong. And therefore the conclusion reached does not hold water. If it sometimes proves correct, it is by accident and not by exegesis.

The model must be that of a single-factor equation. We should try to understand the relationship of Jesus to our own situation with the data furnished us by exegesis. Having reached an understanding of this, we may then ask ourselves what inspiration it gives us for our own situation. We shall use the same example to point out the difference in method. In his historical situation of a stable social context, the Jesus of the gospels seems to emphasize the "short-range" love of neighbor, the giving of direct help, as the parable of the Good Samaritan seems to clearly indicate. Actually, this sort of charity was quite effective within that social context. Jesus proclaimed the good news and the need for conversion in categories that were predominantly interpersonal.

The basic force of oppression in that day was the domination exercised by the law and the religious structures that the religious masters of Israel had imposed on the people. Jesus opposed them vigorously, to the point of becoming a revolutionary threat. This means that the predominantly interpersonal message of Jesus and his criticism of the religious apparatus were seen to be the most effective formulations of transforming love. Jesus adopted this praxis boldly. For the limited context in which he lived, the Roman Empire was not the *punctum dolens,* and it would have been an act of alienation to fight against it as the Zealots did. For the Zealots allowed the more oppressive force to continue functioning through the agency of the Pharisees and other religious power groups.[63]

An understanding of this situation leads us on to the central question: How shall we, in our own situation, most effectively realize charity? If we live in an age when both sin and love have adopted formulations that are increasingly more social, political, and structural, then our charity will have to take on these forms of expression. If interpersonal relationships become more and more dependent on the structures, then it is only by changing the structures that we shall achieve our goals. With this as our point of departure, we conclude that a true comprehension of Christ will bring us to a concrete approach that is quite different from his. And yet we are being more faithful than ever to him.

This example should help us to exercise discernment through the reading of the gospel. When we are confused, stumbling from one position to another, the risk of distortion in interpreting the gospel assumes major proportions. Only an understanding of the total situation can help us over this impasse.

Ambiguity in Church Tradition

Our perplexity has another basis in church tradition. In this tradition it is not easy to distinguish between that which is an expression of the action of the Holy Spirit—so that it would have a normative significance to us—and that which pays tribute to a contemporary ideology.

In the process of political discernment we frequently confront situations where there is a conflict of class interests. We then feel perplexed. There is an ecclesiastical reticence toward everything that involves conflict and class struggle. This is partly because of a mistaken understanding. It is often thought that class struggle is a tactic used to induce change, that it does not yet exist and that one tries to create for the purpose of changing the socio-politico-economic situation. Rather, class struggle is a datum of reality, interpreted by a dialectical sociology.

Class struggle has its origin, from the economic point of view, in the antagonistic position of various classes as well as in the conflict between their interests. To speak of class struggle is to try to understand social reality by observing the position that social classes occupy in the system of social production. This is quite independent of our own emotional and volitional status.[64] Whether or not this struggle exists does not depend on us, but whether it is to continue, or to be aggravated, or to be overcome does depend on us.

Discernment has to take this realistic approach. It cannot dismiss it, because this would interfere with the choice of mediations. Hugo Assmann calls our attention to the false notion that class struggle is a ubiquitous and eternal reality, a problem unavoidable by its very nature, perhaps even a mystical substitute for divine providence. This misconception is rooted in an ignorance of the historically concrete nature of "class struggle" and of the very category of "classes" in Marxist thinking.[65]

The major challenge to our discernment is to see the process of conflict between class interests through the eyes of charity, of transformative love, not allowing ourselves to adopt the ideology that in taking our position on the side of the oppressed we are expressing "hatred" for oppressors. The cause of the situation of oppression, and therefore of the conflict of interests, is the pole of domination, not the oppressed. They are suffering. We have to be on the side of the oppressed in the sense of seeking to improve their condition. But our concern dare not be transformed into a pathological cult of the poor, which would "objectify" the poor and make of them something to satisfy our guilty consciences.

In our efforts to find corrections, both of the biblical hermeneutic and of our understanding of church tradition, we may find the light to clarify our hesitations. In our treatment of criteria (Part Three) we shall consider some factors to help clarify this type of discernment.

The Reasoning Faith of "Logical Thinkers"

Here we have none of the clarity of the mystics and prophets, or the anxieties and doubts of "existentialists." "Logical thinkers" hover over the situation from a relaxed vantage point. There are no motions or emotions. No intuitions. There is only our ability to reason logically.

Nevertheless, this is not a realm of *pure* reason, a happy homeland of solitary intellect. This is not an illuministic, autonomous reason that sets itself up as the last court of appeal. It is a reason coupled with faith. It presupposes an illumination through faith, through revelation, through church tradition. It is a bringing-together of a list of all the reasons we can muster for or against a political mediation. In the presence of this set of arguments a "reading" of faith is made. And it becomes decisive.

Many take this "rationalistic" approach, relying fully on the clairvoyance of intellectual and logical processes. This would not be *spiritual* discernment. "Logical" arguments are deeply impregnated with interests that revelation is not allowed to judge.

There are two serious problems with this approach. The first is the relationship between the force of accumulated arguments, especially when examined through the "lens" of effectiveness, and the spirit of the gospel. The second problem has to do with a better explanation of the relationship between faith and politics.

In the first case, there is the practical question of choosing a mediation. We are concerned that it be effective in making the "general intention," the "utopian objective," a concrete reality. Our reasons are brought forth with this in mind. It is in connection with such a set of arguments favoring the effectiveness of a mediation that spiritual discernment is exercised. The reasons given must be examined in the light of faith. What does this mean?

It would seem to be taking the wrong path to elaborate a theology of Christian effectiveness—for example, the effectiveness or ineffectiveness of the cross—and use this as the starting point for concrete mediations. This would be embarking on a theologico-political odyssey, an odyssey full of dangers, of trial and error. Generally speaking, an abstract theology of effectiveness serves to glorify some ineffectiveness, basing it on the weakness of the cross of Christ and on certain passages of the gospels. How abstract and removed from reality this can be! Furthermore, it fails to perceive that to which reality is tributary. The routing has to be from politics to theology and back again to politics. We have to adopt mediations for their concrete, political effectiveness, and thus we may only ask what our faith has to say about *this concrete effectiveness*.

Arguments on the effectiveness of a mediation have to be seen in the light of the objective. There is an ideological assumption that effectiveness is to be understood only in the light of a society of consumption and competition. A system based on profit is aimed directly at increasing production as such, and effectiveness is seen in terms of a lesser or greater ratio between the means employed and the product obtained. Effectiveness, productivity, profitability are found in the same line of comprehension. This comprehension needs to be dealt with so that the effectiveness of arguments is correctly interpreted. For the *a priori* assumption of all this is the interest of those who possess the means of production. Effectiveness, read in the light of faith, must be understood from the standpoint of service, the cause of the kingdom, the realization of the utopian objective.

Mass and Minority

It is very important in this regard to reflect on the mechanisms of mass and minority.[66] There is a law of the economy of energy that we see operating all the way from the level of inanimate matter to the level of human and societal relationships. According to this law, mechanisms of the economy of energy (mass) become necessary in order for us to have initiatives of a richer synthesis (minority). The mass mechanisms make possible the minority mechanisms, and the latter exercise the function of dealing with the "massifying," negative tendencies inherent in the mass mechanisms. The minority is characterized by its ability to achieve immunity from mass tendencies. On the other hand, without the mass mechanisms the minority could not exist. Any utopian project has to respect this dialectic: to have mass mechanisms that have a different sort of effectiveness from minority initiatives. Effectiveness has to be interpreted in line with this dialectic. At all levels one finds the masses and the elite. Each level exists in the midst of mass and elite factors, so that there can be a functioning of the mechanisms of the economy of energy (mass) or to make decisions that require higher energy levels (the minority).

Decisions that get beyond the immediacy of mass mechanisms to find long-range solutions are typically those of the minority. On the other hand, the use of mechanisms that exempt us from personal decisions and that set up structures benefiting humanity follows a mass approach. In any case, enormous energy is required to discover benefits that go beyond the immediate horizon of the present situation. Otherwise, it is sufficient to follow the normal flow of institutional rhythm that has been created. There are two types of effectiveness here. Both are necessary, but in different initiatives and different proportions. Discernment is operative in the search for an optimum proportion, to the extent that we can perceive it.

It may be that what is wrong with a pastoral letter that takes as its only criterion of effectiveness (and therefore decisive in the choice of mediations) that all new structures must be accepted, consciously and openly, by all, may be just this nonperception of the mass/minority duality. A minority model will never work for the masses. Mass mechanisms must be created that will not be so mass-productive as to dehumanize. Here is where minority action enters the picture. Jesus himself used mass mechanisms in his preaching. Is not his categorization of the kingdom of God an instance of it? On the other hand, the gospels contain a number of minority demands.

A reading of the works of J. L. Segundo, cited above, will round out our cursory examination inspired by his works. Awareness of the mass/minority dualism is of the utmost importance in the discernment of mediations and helps us to avoid a certain purism in our choice of mediations. It keeps us from thinking that only minority mediations are evangelical, that the only Christian effectiveness is that of the minority, in disregard of mass mediations and mass effectiveness. For these mediations reach persons through mechanisms that exempt them from endless decision-making, which would lead to exhaustion. In fact, it would make human life impossible.

Relationships of Faith and Politics

The problem of the relationship between faith and politics is as old as Christianity. If it has not always been treated theoretically, it has at least been present in pragmatic responses revealing an ideological posture. Today it has been presented in a fresh way on the Latin American continent.

Here we must consider a matter of a more generic nature. Any theory that is founded on something essential to human life cannot be suppressed as long as that need continues. There are three fundamental needs of human beings that must be confronted by correlative sciences in an attempt to work out solutions. But inasmuch as these needs are integral parts of the same human being, there is a risk of reducing these three levels of needs to just one level, or at any rate giving prominence to one and making the others secondary.

The three levels are:
- the need for material goods to sustain life, to be met by economic theory;
- a need at the level of social relationships, to be solved by political theory;
- the need to explain the fact of death, which is the province of theological reasoning.

Thus we have economics, politics, and faith (or theology). They concern themselves with the three basic levels of human existence.

Each of these fields can easily be invaded by another. Thus, when seeking a solution to the problem of death, when the response is made at the level of material goods there is an invasion of theology by economics; or when this problem is put in the framework of purely historical social relationships, then politics supplants faith. The same can happen with faith: it can be made the cure for material problems or those involving social relationships, thus transforming itself into economics and politics. On the other hand, there are close connections between these sectors: the same person lives in all three dimensions.

In this discussion we shall confine ourselves to the relationship between the second level (politics) and the third level (faith). We shall attempt a summary typology of these relationships.[67]

The Substitution Relationship

This type of relationship seeks to substitute one activity for another. In extreme cases, the one activity will completely eliminate the other. In the present case, we have politics being substituted for faith, transforming itself into a religion. It tries to provide an overall solution to human existence in such a way that the enigma of death is resolved by the creation of a utopia, which is the motivating force behind the political objective in question. It leaves no room for a religious response. Politics swallows up faith.

The substitution could take place in the opposite direction: religion is reduced to the level of pure politics. It becomes totally horizontal. It responds to the question of death entirely within the framework of time. It no longer corresponds to a Christian faith, which would of necessity require an eschatological, transcendental approach. In this relationship, the two initiatives try to absorb each other.

The limit and risk of such a relationship is the curtailment of human existence. Because the temporal reality is that which immediately affects persons, and cannot in any case be obviated, whereas the transcendental reality can be perceived only within the temporal framework, what this means is that faith, in this joust of substitution, ends up being suppressed in both cases. When the relationship is that of substitution, the result is always the same: the victory of politics, which sets itself up as a "religion." In practice, a radically politicized faith or a politics that has taken on messianic overtones both amount to the same thing.

It is impossible for faith to absorb politics in the sense that politics becomes "supernatural." In practice what happens is that a "supernatural" realm is sapped of its transcendent reality. Politics masquerades in the name of faith.

This means that we have both bad politics and bad religion. Faith is ideologized and we unwittingly come to think that it is being experienced in its pure form.

The Synthesis Relationship

This type of relationship involves the disappearance of the two activities in favor of a third, in the Hegelian sense of *Aufhebung* (eradication, preservation, and sublimation at the same time). In practice, this does not differ very much from the previous position, but it involves a very different concept. Here politics does not replace faith, or vice versa, but a dialectical view of history is adopted wherein the two dimensions are imperfect factors in a synthesis. At a certain point, a new synthesis is worked out, so that the two levels are absorbed into a *tertium quid novum* that cancels out the two previous factors, retaining the valid features of both in a new form.

This is the Marxist view of this relationship, where both politics and religion are to be absorbed into new socio-economic relationships. The relationship between politics and faith has been a false one, deriving from the alienated situation in which persons have been living. Once this condition has been superseded, the relationship disappears. Whatever is human and genuine in the old system will be absorbed into the new socio-economic relationships.

The earlier relationship thus ceases to exist. It is a prediction based on a Marxist view of reality. It hides behind an anthropology and a philosophy that fundamentally contradicts the Christian view of human nature. Its cancellation presupposes that faith is an ideological element of the state apparatus, which will disappear once this type of state has disappeared. It is a negation, pure and simple, of human transcendence. Thus it is a relationship that eviscerates faith, because its presuppositions include the denial that faith is an authentic feature of human existence.

Here, unquestionably, is the reason for the reservation that many Christians feel toward participating in any activity that puts them in close proximity to Marxists. Inasmuch as many features of a Christian's concrete faith are in fact ideological, the Christian is tempted to identify that faith with a simple ideological justification for a system that should be suppressed.

The Subordination Relationship

In this relationship the two activities are maintained, but one is made hierarchically superior and dominant in relation to the other. This domination may at times be that of faith over politics, at other times that of politics over faith. In the Middle Ages these two elements could be identified with Caesaropapism and clericalism. These two movements have long since been studied in depth and have been critically rejected. But this does not prevent us from reliving the problems at the practical level in our own time.

The modern state, especially in those areas where Christianity is the religion of the masses, is concerned with putting faith at the service of its own plans. The new form of "national security" ideology, which is very potent in Latin America, has as its global strategy the concept of geopolitics. Religion, which in the Latin American context is almost exclusively represented by the Roman Catholic Church, is seen by geopolitics as something to be manipulated. In this model for society there is a definite subordination of faith to the purposes of the state.

Clericalism, it seems, is on its last legs. Even where it is still in evidence, we see only vestiges of a disappearing phenomenon. Faith in the role of a subordinator belongs to a sacral world that the process of secularization has been dismantling ever since it came into existence. In certain parts of Latin America one may observe certain phenomena and manifestations where the Christian and, more concretely, the clergyman has a decisive word to say concerning politics. Nevertheless, these are fringe areas and clericalism is on the way to extinction.

The Coexistence Relationship

In this relationship faith and politics are independent of each other, with friendly or hostile relationships to the other, depending on the concrete situation. Each, at least theoretically, recognizes the autonomy and the independent right of existence of the other. Here is the classic case of the modern pluralist state where religion is specialized, personalized, and restricted to a well-defined sector. Thomas Luckmann's analysis reveals a trend toward secularized states. The official models of religion have been losing their universal, obligatory plausibility, to become instead products offered on the free-enterprise market. Every religious view has its place in the democratic, pluralist sun of modern liberal society.[68]

Complaints arise over practical issues that have to do with either faith or politics invading the territory of the other, going beyond the boundaries of its sphere. At the theoretical level there is a mutual recognition that serves as a tranquilizing backdrop to the understanding of society. The basic characteristic of this position is the personalization of faith. It involves a renunciation of incarnation in political mediations and a restriction to purely spiritual and religious domains. Concretely, it is a traditional or renewed Catholicism that is dedicated to sacramental and devotional practices and stays out of touch with the political sphere. It agrees well with the Catholicism of the Cursillo movement: "The Cursillos of Christianity movement is not a political movement. It is not and does not propose to be a political party. It does not intervene in the struggle between political parties. It does not prepare its people directly for politics. The Cursillo movement is detached from politics; it is above and beyond party politics."[69]

This position is clearly opposed to the theology of liberation. Its political neutrality is only apparent: it relies for its pseudoneutrality on the dominant forces of the established order. The apoliticism of faith is an illusion and is part of a bourgeois ideology that has no intention of being questioned by faith.

The Nonreductive Dialectico-Existential Involvement Relationship

This is the view worked out by the theology of liberation, especially by Gustavo Gutiérrez, to explain the relationship between faith and politics, because none of the above approaches are considered satisfactory.

Faith, as a higher level, has a many-sided influence on the lower level of politics. It is the foundation of politics, its source of significance and dynamism working toward full realization, an enlivening and criticizing principle. The level of politics, however, is that critical locus where faith is verified. Faith does not exist except in the realization of lower levels, in this case politics, and the existence of this lower level is already a partial, provisional realization (yet quite necessary) of a reality that transcends its own boundaries.[70]

This is not the *substitution* relationship: both levels continue in existence. Political mediations retain their proper consistency. Faith is expressed through these mediations. They do not become "religious." Nor do mediations become a substitute for faith; faith is not exhausted by them. It plays a critical role. It gives advance notice of the caducity, the fragility, and the limitations of these mediations, proclaiming the fact that they are being continually superseded until total victory is gained over sin, death, and injustice. This is not the *synthetic* relationship: the process is not immanent to history, is not the fruit of a circumscribed dialectic, but is the dialectical interaction of freedoms where the free action of God's grace, which transcends any immanent dialectic, is not ignored. Nor is this a matter of *subordination:* political mediations are secular and autonomous, with a consistency of their own. Faith becomes visible by means of them. It does not subordinate them. They are chosen at a given moment as the concrete, historical expression of faith. There is no parallel *coexistence* here: there is no dualism of a Platonic rootage, in the final analysis. Rather, reality is understood as a unique salvation history in which human and divine freedoms interact.

Thus there is a nonreductive involvement where faith is expressed in political mediations chosen in the *hic et hunc* of history but is by no means exhausted by them. This is parallel with the Chalcedonian schema of *inconfuse et indivise* with respect to the relationship between Jesus Christ's humanity and divinity.[71]

This new understanding of the relationship between faith and politics in Latin America has intimate connections with the reality of the historical meaning of Christianity and the church. Latin America is made up of nations where the human masses subsist at a low level of historical consciousness and where the degree of consensus is at a very low level. Christianity is proclaimed as the "people of God," and the Catholic Church is thought to be one of its fuller realizations in history. It cannot content itself with being just a culture with traditions, rites, customs, symbols, vocabulary, themes, and social gestures. Such gestures must of necessity reflect the life and consciousness of a free people. Basic to "being the church" and deriving by necessity from the preaching of the central message of the gospel is the dimension of freedom to be constituted as the "people of God."

Thus a part of the new praxis of the church is the struggle for human rights and a critical appraisal of the models of development. In this new praxis the church insists on having a sphere of freedom so that it may not only *speak of* freedom but *appeal to* the freedom of persons and may call them *(ekklesia)* to be constituted as a "free people," as a sign of salvation (the church). Without freedom, the persons involved cannot constitute a people. Without a people there is no church. The present oppressive situation keeps Latin Americans in the status of masses and does not permit the formation of a people. This is why there is an anti-people, anti-Church situation. And the task of liberation, to be carried out by denunciation and proclamation in both words and deeds, is not just one among many tasks of the church, but is its new, unavoidable praxis if it wants to be the church.[72]

The universal church, under the influence of the Latin American bishops, in solemn declarations of two Synods of Bishops, has adopted the praxis of denouncing unjust situations involving the basic rights of the human person (Synod of 1971); its mission includes the defense and promotion of the dignity and fundamental rights of the human person (same Synod). At the Synod of 1974, in a message to the peoples of the world, mention is made of a ministry of the church to promote human rights.

This represents a general approach that, to be made concrete, will of necessity have political consequences, because the violation of these rights is intimately bound up with the economic and political models offered by the various governments. The church of today does not understand its mission if it does not relate to this new type of praxis, which implies political stances. In fact, there is the real possibility that political attitudes may be used, contrary to the church's wishes, for movements that oppose many of its own ideas. This is no deterrent for adopting political attitudes. Just because others may abuse a correct response does not mean that it should not be made. The guilt does not lie with the respondent but with whatever has created the unjust situation being contested. Its instigators are the ones who have favored the existence of movements that have power to take unfair advantage of the presence and action of the church. There should be no illusions about this.[73]

To shirk this task of defending human rights, freedom, and liberation of the oppressed is to neglect the basic function of the contemporary Latin American church. It means accepting the thesis of so many contemporary Latin American governments, according to which the role of the church is to maintain, within an outer shell of Christian words and deeds, the nonexistence of true Christianity and the true church, which cannot make peace with a government that suppresses freedom, justice, and charity.

Only from within the perspective of this relationship between faith and politics in the Latin American setting can the process of discernment take place with any real clarity. The reasoning faith of "logical thinkers" cannot reason away the mutually implicative, existential nature of faith and politics. Thus political decisions, for us, do not derive simply from ideological options chosen by political parties, but in line with a Christian view that follows a pattern of politics-to-theology-to-politics. Politics provides us with socioanalytical factors. Theology reads these factors in the light of revelation. It returns, in the third phase of the formula, to make a political decision. Discernment follows precisely this formula. The difference between a politician, as a politician, and a Christian is in the presence or absence of the mediation of faith between the first and third phases of the formula. The politician engages in discernment for political action on the basis of politics. The hermeneutic mediation of revelation does not intervene. The Christian—for example, as a member of a religious congregation—who engages in spiritual discernment allows faith to intervene at its place in the formula. This intervention is no substitute for the first or third phases. The socio-analytical factors derive from the political sciences. The decisions are made within the context of politics. Faith acts in interpreting the data provided by social analysis and thus influences the type of option that then takes place in the political realm.

This third method of discernment puts the accent on a pure relationship between politics and faith. It seeks to avoid in particular the mistakes made through the substitution of politics for faith. It will never become an instrument of analysis. It is the interpretation of the results of a socio-political reading with the key of revelation. From this interpretation arises a Christian awareness of reality that will then help the Christian to make concrete decisions, to choose the mediation that best fits the situation.

Summary

There are three types or modes of discernment. They correspond to three perceptions of the relationship between objective reality and subjective conditioning. Identifying the dialectical relationship between the "general intention" and the "concrete mediation" is achieved in three different ways. In each case, there is a positive aspect and a potential risk.

The first method has about it a certainty, a clarity, a calm perception of the demands of the gospel. It lacks the anxiety of hesitation, as well as the need to pursue a slow process of logical reasoning. This was the experience of Paul, who was converted from an attitude of persecuting the church to being its great apostle. God appeared to him as to "one of abnormal birth" (1 Cor. 15:8), with the enormous graciousness of totally undeserved favor. This is the universe of grace, of charism, of the identifiable presence of the Lord.

This type of discernment is experienced by persons involved in, and situations relating to, an extraordinary intensity of interest and action. Elements deriving from the deep individual or collective unconscious can pose a profound threat to such a choice. The risk involved is the illusion of reading God's blueprint where all that exists is a surreptitious self-seeking.

The second type is that of an oscillating search among alternatives. This takes time. It results from a more detailed observation of the internal life of an individual or group. Time provides greater assurance of certainty. This mode of discernment seeks to avoid hasty, extreme decisions, so as to experience the presence of God's Spirit in the interaction of joys and sorrows, of consolations and disappointments. This experience is especially enhanced by confrontation with the life of Jesus, formula of inspiration for great undertakings.

The limitations and risk of this approach have to do with the suspense involved, the long, enervating intervals of indecision in reliance on a nonprobative biblical hermeneutic. In the name of ongoing discernment one may indefinitely prolong decisions that have become quite urgent. It could become an excuse for not adopting a more radical decision. This is especially true at the group level. The lack of clarity could ultimately lead to continuing with the status quo. A change in position becomes more difficult.

The third type of discernment has the advantage of controllable reasoning. Outsiders can assist in the weighing and discussing of arguments. A highly rational clarity can be achieved, presupposing an interpretation of faith.

We Westerners are very sophisticated in the game of discussion. We are highly skilled in "fencing" with ideas. It is all too easy for us to transform discernment into an open-ended series of "rationalizations," where an intelligence aligned with unacknowledged interests can find an abundance of ways to falsify the meaning of discernment. We can lose ourselves in theoretical discussions on effectiveness, faith, and politics without ever taking up the concrete mediations that would lead to real change.

All three of these modes of discernment are human. None of them possesses divine certainty. We must always assume an attitude of humility in our search, relying on the help of colleagues who, like us, search, with unfeigned desire, for the most appropriate mediations for establishing the kingdom of God in history, in the midst of the ambiguities of that history. We have no choice other than this painful effort to see clearly, and to make decisions in the light of that clarity.

PART THREE

CRITERIA FOR DISCERNMENT

The three types or modes of choosing a mediation can be tested by criteria. These help us to have a clearer understanding of the action of the Spirit and to protect ourselves, to the extent that human weakness permits, from mistaking our own will, our own capriciousness, for the will of God. The criteria are meant to help us to read reality through spiritual eyes, in the light of revelation, so that we may perceive the difference between the will of God, grace, and justice on the one hand, and our own selfishness, petty interests, and individual and social sins on the other.

We shall be dealing here with theological criteria. This means that discernment is to be interpreted with the key of faith. This is the key that is given to us by revelation; we accept it as a gift from the Lord, as truth, as holiness. Data deriving from our common sense and from the human sciences are reviewed at a secondary level through spiritual eyes. We use the term "spiritual" here to refer to the world of grace, the order of salvation, the supernatural plane. There is no dualism here, but two distinct levels at which the one reality is interpreted. There is only one reality: grace and sin, the salvific will of God and the sinful opposition of antagonistic forces. This one reality can be inter-

preted by various tools of analysis. The one we are using here is that offered by theology. And our purpose is to accurately define where salvation is taking place and where an action is sin, so that we may adopt salvific mediations and not those that lead to condemnation.

We must distinguish between two types of criteria: subjective and objective. The first type has reference to the condition of the subject—individual or group—that is to perform the process of discernment. It seeks to discover what happens to this agent (subject) and, starting from there, to attempt, by using the key of faith, to understand the action of God. The second type, by contrast, has reference to the objective mediations under consideration; it reads them in the light of the demands of faith.

Chapter VII

Subjective Criteria

Potentialities of the Subject

The first criterion can be discovered in Mark 2:27: "The Sabbath was made for the sake of man and not man for the Sabbath." The problem is this: an individual or group agent is confronted with a concrete mediation. This mediation corresponds to a utopian objective that is to be incarnated. The problem is posed, concretely, to the agent, the subject. The first step will have to be a realistic assessment of the psycho-social capacities of the agent for realizing this mediation.

Every individual and every group has a history. An effort must be made to become aware of the past of this person or group, using the analytical resources available. Of importance here are the opinions of other persons who are not directly involved in the discernment but who have some knowledge either of the agent or of the mediation in question. Such persons, because of their distance and impartiality, may think things through with the agent of discernment, sizing up the goal and the consequences of the decision for those involved. The mediation is made for, tailored to, the group; the group does not exist for the sake of the mediation. The group has a certain specific capacity. In other words, no one should be obligated to do the impossible. Today, given a more extensively elaborated psychological reading, we are in a better position to understand this gospel passage. Every individual or group has a certain level of resistance. Anything that goes beyond that threshhold could crush the subject and lead to serious consequences.

A criterion is subjective insofar as it refers to the potentialities of subjects—individuals or groups—bound as they are to their own existential history. In the final analysis the verification of this will also depend on the individual or group. And we must appropriate all the available data in order to arrive at an awareness of our "resistance potential." We will never arrive at a degree of certainty that does not involve some element of risk.

When dealing with mediations of a political nature, we should be informed of the level of education necessary for adopting such measures. At the moment it may be that the subject is not sufficiently mature to adopt a political mediation. But through a program of apprenticeship the individual or group might eventually qualify. It may be that the decision reached through discernment will be to postpone a decision. There is nothing incongruous about this, provided we do not stop at this point. If a mediation has been seen as desirable, and its realization is recognized as impossible merely because the necessary psycho-social conditions do not exist at the moment, then the process of discernment should deal with the means for creating such conditions. One may have to draw the difficult conclusion that this is an utter impossibility and that no way of overcoming the obstacle is foreseeable. In such cases, the process of discernment will be terminated.

A mediation is like the Sabbath: it must lie within the horizon of human potentiality. It cannot become an absolute, to be achieved at *any* cost. The subjective element of such a criterion must not degenerate into an arbitrary subjectivism. The validity of such a criterion presupposes a basic honesty, without which no discernment can take place. Nor may the subject become an absolute. The subject must be seen in its historical and dialectical relationship to the mediation. Both make demands. The mediation demands an effort on the part of the subject, the agent, to make it happen. The agent requires of the mediation that it be human in scope, something that can be done in the historical here and now.

Returning to the gospel passage, we may enlarge upon it by saying: "The Sabbath was made for the sake of man and not man for the Sabbath; nevertheless the Sabbath calls man to account." Historical mediations have been made to our mold, but they also demand that we ready ourselves to accept them. In the absence of this perspective of a mutual interaction we would give way to the extremes of either an overbearing subjectivism or an oppressive rigorism.

The Existence of Support Structures

Our adoption of concrete mediations requires our commitment, the giving of ourselves. This act of self-donation, whose ultimate origin is to be found in the interaction between the gift of God's freedom and our free response, requires a socio-structural undergirding if it is to resist the ravages of time. We do not consist of pure subjectivity or pure freedom. We relate dialectically to social structures.

What we are and what we want to be has to be said and heard not just in our words alone but also in the credibility of the structures we seek to erect. There is no individual or group that can survive in the awareness that they can find no legitimizing structures and defenses against threats in the society around them. We have a horror of chaos. It is the unthinkable. It is a profound threat to us. And our decisions, when they do not find social support, face just this sort of threat. They are confronted with the chaos that derives from an absence of any corroboration for their existence.

Our life is a continual effort to organize past events into an ordered and meaningful whole. Each new option, each new mediation, must be integrated into this universe, even though it necessitates some reformulation of its significance. We seek consistency, fragile as it may be, in the data that have been accumulated and stored on the various shelves of our personal history. The same process takes place with a group also.

This continuum goes on receiving fresh stimuli from new elements from outside us, from the external and internal environment, through a process of conscientization. This is a vulnerable process, threatened at each moment by factors that could cause discontinuity. No individual or group attains perfect integration of all the elements in its biographical makeup. It will never be in perfect harmony and consonance with what the social structures are saying to it. There is always that degree of dissatisfaction that contains within it the origin of all change.

Thus if we adopt a concrete mediation, especially where this means an important change of lifestyle, and if we do not find support in external structures, we feel our solidarity threatened. We have a horror of social nonacceptance, of nonintegration into some social context. This feeling of being aliens, foreign to the environment, puts our option in tension, and over the long haul we find it difficult to bear.

A biographical definition or a political option demands a state of continuity or the existence of either a homogeneous majority surrounding it or a meaningful minority to protect it. This is because we find our own meaning in the context of our environment. If that environment is adverse to us, we begin to doubt our position. We need continual support, a specific social context that gives its approval to our world of values, our lifestyle. Any meaningful system has a social structure that lends it credibility. It needs this social foundation to continue its existence as a real world inhabited by real human beings. The more significant the supporting structures, the greater the support. The converse is also true: the more important the forces that call us into question, the greater the threat they pose.

Let us suppose, for example, that a group of young persons, in the process of discernment, have chosen a certain mediation. It is of fundamental importance that other persons representative of the value they have chosen give them support. Criticism or mockery could destroy everything. We attach ourselves to those who sustain our positions: we need justification and credibility.

Language plays an important role in this process. We need a "conversational apparatus" that will really articulate what we are thinking and saying. By language, through this conversational apparatus, we appropriate our universe of values, we maintain it, we reinforce our decisions and defend them against ongoing threats. In this way our subjectivity, the interiorization of our decisions, takes on substance and consistency. We make our decisions meaningful by integrating them into the value system of our society. We triumph over chaos. We bring order to our existence.

These reflections will help us see the importance of a dialectical relationship between what we decide and what we are experiencing socially. And what does this have to do with a subjective criterion of discernment?

For a decision to be viable, the subject—individual or group—must be in possession of circumstances that permit them to perform it and live it over a long period of time. If these conditions are not present, we have a criterion for advising against the action, dampening our enthusiasm for it. The conditions that provide for a structure of credibility are: legitimation, therapy, control.

Legitimation

The function of legitimation is to show that the mediation decided upon has a right to existence, to "citizenship" in our society. There is a kind of "pretheoretical" legitimation deriving from the simple fact of the tacit, de facto acceptance of the mediation as a consequence of its very existence. The mere existence of any reality already gives it legitimacy until it is negated or destroyed. In everyday language we would say: "That's the way things are." Expressions such as this seek to justify what exists by virtue of the very fact of its existence. In many cases this is all that is needed, especially for phenomena that fit easily into the overall system and cause no problems. Generally speaking, this is the legitimation of many of our choices. We choose a mediation. No one says anything against it. There is no opposition. It makes no changes in the general scheme of things, and peace reigns. It becomes legitimate merely by its presence.

There is another, deeper level of legitimation: the incipient theoretical phase. Generally speaking this takes place by means of popular sayings, myths, legends, folk tales, phrases that everyone repeats, slogans, proverbs, quotations of famous persons. In the world of religion it takes place by means of religious sayings, some taken from sacred scripture, often completely out of context. They find use as isolated, legitimating logia. Others will appeal to some spiritual tradition that is following its course. Here there is ideological interaction.

Frequently the saying is interpreted and used within a well-defined ideology. Someone, for example, is confronted with a decision to help others: innumerable hours of his or her time will be spent in consoling the afflicted, without any perspective beyond the stringent limits of an I-thou relationship. As legitimation, sayings such as the following are given: "The soul has infinite value . . . Christ died for these people . . . all are the children of God and merit our help," and the like.

A third level of legitimation is the fully elaborated theoretical phase. It may be that the previous levels have been inadequate, either because clear objections to the target mediation are hovering in the air or because we have a disinterested, critical awareness that does not permit us to be satisfied with these other levels of legitimation. This kind of thinking—theology, in the case of spiritual discernment—gives rise to arguments, reflections, more sophisticated and profound lines of reasoning, so as to legitimate one's choice. To continue with our example, we elaborate a theology of charity from biblical themes, from church tradition, or from the thoughts of modern theologians. The greater the person's claim, and the more critical the position, the more elaborate a theory will be required. The theology of liberation will in this sense exercise the function of legitimation for the choice of mediations of a socio-political nature; a conservative theology, conversely, will justify the apolitical stance of many decisions.

At this level of thought, theology has a legitimating function. In the area of discernment, it is of great importance. In such systems it performs the role of an ideology. And within the environment of the church this type of legitimation is of great value. It explains why theological discussions sometimes take on a polemical tone. The case of Bishop Lefebvre exemplifies how a traditional theology serves as a great legitimizer of conservative options in the field of liturgy, politics, and so forth. And the theology of Vatican II is the legitimizing basis for innovations introduced into the postconciliar church. These two theologies are on a collision course—two different sources of legitimation for diametrically opposed decisions.

It is important that the mediation that grows out of our discernment should receive legitimation at this third level. And to the extent that it finds such a source of legitimacy it will be more likely to find support. As to options in the field of socio-political mediations, involving greater proximity to the poor and oppressed and in their defense, there are sources of legitimation at all three levels. The existence of options already made along this line (first level); a series of pronouncements and recurrent expressions, such as: church of the poor, church born among the poor, church of Medellín (second level); and the theoretical elaboration of the theology of liberation, pontifical documents, bishops' conferences, and the like (third level). This work must be continued so that options may be supported, and so that those who embark upon these options will not feel isolated, cut off from the church. On the contrary, the more that the presence of the church is felt, the more legitimation there is, and the greater the possibility of persevering in these options. This is a valuable contribution that Latin American theologians can make to a change of options in their part of the world.

To the extent that liberation praxis needs theory for its justification and legitimation, to this extent it will be threatened by the chaos of irrelevance, by the obscurity of doubts and uncertainty. It is a work that has to be brought to completion, by a shoulder-to-shoulder collaboration of praxis and theory, in a mutually enriching interaction.

As far as religious congregations are concerned, chapters and official documents play a fundamental role in legitimizing the options of groups of religious. Various congregations have at last approved texts that reflect a position and consciousness in which liberation is accentuated. We may not minimize these documents, speaking of them as so much paper. Even if within the congregation these documents do not go beyond the norm of real experience, and even if no concrete realization is immediately evident, their mere existence has enormous significance. It is an ideal basis for legitimizing new experiments. And groups that wish to undertake a concrete incarnation of these texts do not feel threatened by an adverse "conversational apparatus" (language). On the contrary, they have already found a *dialectical* expression of their biographical definition.

For example, it was in this vein that a recent general assembly of the Society of Jesus came forward with an important statement on the *diakonia* of faith

SUBJECTIVE CRITERIA

in the promotion of justice, providing a legitimizing basis that permits groups of Jesuits to launch experiments in the field of liberation. We read such phrases as:

> ... the commitment to promote justice, in solidarity with those we term "voiceless" and "powerless," a commitment imposed upon us by our faith in Jesus Christ and by our mission to proclaim the gospel, prompting us to become accurately informed [analysis of reality] as to the difficult problems of our life together, and then to identify and assume the responsibilities that are specifically ours in the social order [choice of mediation].
>
> Jesuit communities must help each of their members to overcome resistance, fears, and apathy, which hinder the true comprehension of social, economic, and political problems posed within the city, the region, or the nation, or even at the international level.

We could continue with similar quotations. There are some really intense statements. They are the fruit of experiences already lived in some areas, on the one hand, while on the other they serve to set new experiments in motion. Although our life at present falls quite short of what we are saying, yet these statements continue to have the function of questioning and legitimizing a new trend that is to be adopted.

Therapy

The more legitimate a mediation, the more it will experience threats from within and from without. Any dissonance with the social system is a threat. The impossibility of completely assimilating the mediation, the lingering suspicion that inhabits everything that is human, the dissatisfaction derived from being out of phase with our desires, our anxieties, our ideals, and the "unimportance" of the choice we have made, together with factors that oppose it, constitute an ongoing temptation to abandon our decision. They interfere with our discernment. They weaken our convictions. And if the degree of dissatisfaction becomes unbearable, we end up abandoning our option.

As we confront this situation we must create structures that will mitigate this dissatisfaction, that will annul it, or at least reduce its impact. Such structures have a therapeutic function. Every group, if it is to adopt a way of life and action, needs defense mechanisms in order to face the continual crises that come upon it. We must create them for each concrete situation. One of the principal defenses is an awareness that there are others involved in the same adventure as we, an awareness that is fed by communication, meetings, and visits. The more radical, difficult, or arduous a decision, the more need there is to feel the presence of other groups involved in the same risk. True community life is a highly effective therapy. It alleviates tensions, softens hostile blows, and fortifies the spirit.

A portion of our discernment has to do with discovering the practical resources available to neutralize or at least alleviate the tension created by the threats that surround us. Every social system needs therapeutic devices. When we make decisions, especially in the area of politically oriented mediations, we need reinforcement against the accusations, the complaints, the threats that will be made.

The importance of therapy increases to the extent that our decisions represent a minority within the social structure. When we do not receive support from the overall system, then there is all the greater need of creating active and intensive defenses. Along this line, the relevance of meetings, conventions, and workshops becomes apparent. We sometimes hear the criticism that meetings and get-togethers serve no purpose. They are pure "foolishness," nothing but chatter. But the critics overlook the importance of the reinforcement that comes from what seems on the surface to be nothing but words. Here is a real therapy to enliven those who are engaged in the same task. We are encouraged by the impact of the presence of others. And the more emotionally significant the personalities present, the greater the therapeutic force of the meeting.

This consideration, which is more sociological than psycho-individual, finds a theological expression in such a well-known experience as that of the church itself, which from its very beginning has participated around the same table, with the same message, in a sharing of blessings: the converts "met constantly to hear the apostles teach, and to share the common life, to break bread, and to pray. . . . All whose faith had drawn them together held everything in common. . . . With one mind they kept up their daily attendance at the temple, and, breaking bread in private houses, shared their meals with unaffected joy, as they praised God and enjoyed the favor of the whole people" (Acts 2:42–47). In the midst of opposition from Jews and pagans alike, this Christian minority found in its common life an enormous therapy against the threats against it. And it survived.

This oneness of a single heart and soul, to the extent that everything was held in common, had the effect of a "great power" (Acts 4:32–35). Furthermore, these Christians, supported by the strength that this common life gave to them, could not only remain firm but even grow through this very testimony. New groups of Christians and religious novices are well aware of the importance of this support structure.

Social Control

This is yet another support structure, not quite so "innocent" as the others. It becomes more and more operational as legitimation and therapy prove ineffective.

Every social body creates its own controls to defend itself from the incursions of hostile and subversive elements that seek to increase the level of dissatisfaction and thus precipitate changes. Spiritual discernment must to some extent provide its own defenses. In traditional ascetical language we speak of "fleeing the occasions of sin . . . guiding our feelings and hearts . . . avoiding the reading of harmful books . . . avoiding bad companions," and so forth. These are forms of control that serve to defend us from situations that bring questioning and temptation with respect to the values we are defending. Within the structures of the religious life there is a well-devised system of control that operates through the agency of taboos, regulation of travel, censorship of letters, admission of faults, and so on.

Generally speaking, this entire system of control is falling into disrepair. Many persons who are unprepared to confront new situations become victims. There is a certain minimum of control that cannot be relinquished without some degree of irresponsibility. Today, these structures must not be imposed from without, as they once were. This does not mean that they have become unnecessary. They must be established and adopted as a defense that we need at both the personal and group level. But they must be stripped of their unattractive, oppressive features, so that they become a free initiative, based on the candid acknowledgment of our weakness and need of protection. It is not at all childish to recognize that a controlling structure can help us at a given moment. Childishness is fostered by repressive structures that are not internalized but imposed from without. Decision-making and freedom are involved in the creation and adaptation of structures.

The process of discernment thus provides for the existence of support structures that make our choices viable in terms of legitimation, therapy, and social control. Given this combination of socio-structural supports, a decision becomes ratified. In theological terms we could say "grace presupposes nature." The work that God is performing among us presupposes the construction on our part of that which makes grace effective. And these "credibility structures" are the conditions that make grace possible. Hence their importance and necessity for decision-making by the process of discernment.[74]

Internal Composure

The third subjective criterion has to do with the "state of mind" of the individual or group involved in discernment. The presence of God is particularly characterized by peace, by the inner joy that comes from a clear conscience, as opposed to confusion, embittered anxiety, and self-seeking aggressiveness.

Through the movements of the soul we can begin to perceive in what direction the presence of God is moving. There is a kind of healthy anxiety that finds expression in the solicitude we feel for others, in our enthusiasm for justice. This is a sign of God's presence. Anything else is sterile, the fruit of inertia, of perplexity, of a recognition of our own helplessness. Such anxiety does not lead to praxis, to any outgoing activity on our part, to any giving of our lives.

Whenever a group meets in an attitude of freedom, of generosity, of a cheerful willingness to serve others, of a relaxed response to the demands of the kingdom, we may regard these attitudes as signaling the presence of God.

The more radical and more difficult the choice, the more we must experience the presence of this peace and joy. It is a reflection of the compatibility between our psycho-human capabilities and the choice we are making. When these two are out of alignment, the first symptoms will be anxiety, sadness, insecurity, confusion.

Some of the more radical options call for a considerable amount of spiritual energy. When a person or group does not possess this reserve or potential, there will frequently be problematical repercussions at the emotional and sexual levels. The inner tension created by the new situation may trigger a turning to compensations that can have the effect of marring the purity of their public witness. It is easy for them to fall into rationalizations. Under these circumstances, many "free" attitudes are justified and entered into.

There are groups of Christians and religious who opt for a life of greater involvement with the poor and oppressed along lines dictated by social criticism. They have spaded fertile seedbeds of new life in the church. But because many religious and priests end up leaving the religious life and the priesthood, their accomplishments lose much of their force in the church at large.

Without going into the moralistic judgments leveled at their decision, but rather approaching the problem from a social and ecclesiastical standpoint, it is undeniable that damage is done here. What happens will be seized upon as a pretext for the forces of conservatism and reactionism to entrench themselves more deeply in their positions.

It is not my intention to belittle in any way the wider vision of the kingdom of God that these priests and religious have. But there are certain lifestyles that bring discredit in church circles. From a *strategic* point of view, their effect is harmful. There *is* an ecclesiastical reality, and that reality is of importance to the cause of liberation.

As regards the process of discernment, the capacity for psychological and emotional equilibrium must be taken into consideration, especially by groups of priests and religious. We must be aware of the fact that this type of life has demands that cannot be ignored with impunity. Much of what is written about and lived in a "third way" is explained in terms of experiences and situations for which persons were not prepared, which leads to disconcerting reactions and a new round of rationalizations.

These three subjective criteria help us to see the viability of a particular choice as it pertains to the agent of that choice. Basically this is a perception by faith of what God has revealed to us through our own psycho-social structures. In other words, we cannot start with a "theological theory" and then apply it to reality by forcing it to fit. On the contrary, our de facto capacities, created as a part of our individual and social histories at the personal and structural levels, constitute a revelation for us of God's plan in action. Nothing happens outside this context. There is room here for our creativity and freedom, but never outside the given specifics of our own subjectivity and historical conditioning.

This whole field retains a certain degree of elasticity, and there are criteria of other types and objective considerations that can contribute to the process of discernment. When combined with those we have treated thus far, they constitute an adequate basis for an active role in our own history. The gray area is an inescapable fact of human existence, which consists in a continual progress in the direction of a final, eschatological truth.

Confronted with eternity, hesitations disappear. Then we will no longer be in history. Until then, we live in an uncertain quest for decisions that involve freedom, risk, and responsibility.

Chapter VIII

Objective Criteria

It is possible, first of all, for us to fall into the trap already mentioned, of an *a priori,* abstract theoretical elaboration that we then seek to apply to praxis. The elaboration must be dialectical, an interaction between theory (theology) and praxis. Thus this elaboration of the objective criteria by theological methods is not a doctrine ready for application; it is a series of reflections to be confirmed in confrontation with praxis if it is to be seen in its true configuration.

These criteria are found at three levels of theological understanding: in their theological, christological, and ecclesiological relationships. These are three dimensions whose demands must be met in a positive way by a Christian's praxis. They define the objective space of the "mystery" within which the agent of discernment must move in making a choice.[75]

The Theological Dimension

The theological dimension has reference to the "absolute sovereignty of God" over everything that exists. It is the expression of the "Principle and Foundation" of the *Spiritual Exercises* of St. Ignatius. Human beings stand in the presence of God, their Lord, for whose praise, worship, and service they were created. It is from this perspective that everything else is to be considered. It is the expression of God's transcedence that must be present throughout the process of discernment. In whatever choice we make, our eyes must be fixed upon the transcendence of God. It is the light that must illumine us.

This transcendence must not be understood as it has been in traditional

OBJECTIVE CRITERIA 107

thought, as a reality that owes nothing to the world of things and of history, and explains them, giving them meaning and destiny. Until recently this concept was part of our culture, part of our worldview. The world was seen as the "here and now" in opposition to the "hereafter." And science thought that it could find, beyond the phenomena, a substantial essence, certain eternal and absolute laws that would explain the order of creation. In our system of morality it was thought to express the absoluteness of God's will. Today other categories loom prominent on our intellectual horizon: history, existence, a future to be created, movement, development.[76]

Having one's eyes on the transcendence of God is not meant to supply a *total* interpretation of a given reality or situation, whether in the context of "self," of "the group," or of "the objective," but rather presupposes that we are open to what is different, to "the other." The theological dimension of the mystery corresponds to our awareness that all our self-transcendence, whether as an individual or as a group, has its limits. There is therefore a need to maintain a degree of caution in this area. The *concrete* significance of this transcendence will be revealed to us in the christological dimension. The theological aspect keeps us in the suspense of openness, of relativity, of an identity so distant as to maintain us in the expectation of an unending pilgrimage.

Transcendence is never the support of any type of oppression, authoritarianism, power structure, or imposition. Transcendence conceived as power or authority is nothing more than a projection of the human desire to dominate.

The substance of transcendence resides in God. In Old Testament passages especially, a blinding effulgence or glory (*doxa*) introduces the revelation of transcendence. Furthermore, this transcendence stands apart, transforming itself into power for its own use. God is then identified as the one who will not tolerate rivals, "othernesses," and who is prepared to destroy, to remove from his vision, what is different. The plenary truth of God's transcendence is revealed in the face of Christ. "He is the image of God" (2 Cor. 4:4); in his face, the glory of God shines forth (2 Cor. 4:6). Transcendence reaches its peak in humility, in *kenosis,* so that although "the divine nature was his from the first, he did not think to snatch at equality with God, but made himself nothing, assuming the nature of a slave. Bearing the human likeness, revealed in human shape, he humbled himself" (Phil. 2:6-8).

Thus this "keeping an eye on transcendence" does not pull us away from history or from the world, but rather shows up the elements of arrogance and inconsistency in this world and in history, when individuals try to make them absolutes, "a projection of their understanding of transcendence."

The eschatological approach—the approach of hope—is understood as an expression of transcendence. "But we have his promise, and look forward to new heavens and a new earth, the home of justice" (2 Peter 3:13). This is a dimension that helps us to discern in a given mediation its reference to a continuous self-transcendence that is manifested not in its lack of seriousness and consistency but in its openness and persistent questioning. At the theological level, this criterion is somewhat generic; it is a dimension that takes on greater concreteness in the dimensions that follow: the christological and the ecclesiological. And because there is no attempt here to establish a codified or canonical criteriology, the level of reflection cannot help suffering from a certain degree of abstractness. Nevertheless, it is important to keep this dimension in view during the act of discernment.

The eschatological criterion rejects the vaunted self-sufficiency of "all-conquering" reason so dear to the modern mind, thus unmasking its oppresiveness. The liberating dimension lies in an awareness of the way in which human mediations suffer from the temptation to be intolerant of "otherness." The eschatological approach that has been so overworked by European-style political theology and the theology of hope leaves us dissatisfied, inasmuch as with it, we are not exercising our discernment within the context of concrete mediations.

The eschatological dimension of theology must be present in the discernment process as a constant awareness, as a kind of alarm system, rather than as a model to be copied. It is an awareness that performs its function, negatively, by excluding mediations that are bound to the acquisitive instinct and the desire to dominate individuals and groups. Generally speaking, these criteria function more readily in the role of exclusion than that of discovery. But the excluding motif may also perform a creative function by arousing our imagination, forcing it to attempt a rebellion, a refusal to take no for an answer.

Another aspect of the theological dimension is an understanding of the primacy of "divine service" in our decisions. Ignatius is fond of repeating, in his *Exercises,* the important criterion of "service to his Divine Majesty." A goal related to this is that of obtaining salvation for oneself. At first glance this could seem to be a utilitarian criterion and thus opposed to the transcendental aspect of "divine service." But salvation is the highest form of divine service, what Father Henrique Vaz calls the loving restoration, in praise and worship of God, of our own being (supernaturalized), which is seen as the fruit of thankfulness for divine love.[77]

The praxis of charity has to do with the way in which we serve and glorify God. This becomes clearer in the light of the biblical and patristic tradition of the "glory of God." It has a richness that the notion of the praise of God does not duplicate. The glory of God is the divine goodness that expands into the trinitarian processions, in such a way that his omnipotent benevolence communicates to his creatures an image of his perfection. Thus in a secondary way the glory of God is in the image of the divine life received by his creatures. This is why anything that increases the image of divine goodness communicated to God's creatures contributes to the glory of God. This occurs every time that humans act upon God's gifts and cause them to bear fruit in their deeds. In short, the praxis of charity, as an act that transforms the world along the lines of greater justice and love, is the glory of God.[78]

The term "praxis of charity" has been introduced to take away from the term "charity" the emotional tone and strictly private connotation that a bourgeois mentality has given it. This is not the kind of love that goes on condoning an unjust situation, failing to deal with it at its roots. The theological dimension has to be understood in the sense that "divine service," the "glory of God," "salvation" and "charity" are really in effect only when they are altering the present oppressive situation, restoring to the poor their dignity and independence, putting them in a position to live out their freedom. The term "praxis" is used to remove "charity" from the orbit of mere gentility, of simple, interpersonal "niceness," and stations it instead in the real universe: action, the transformation of social relationships.[79]

The transcendent nature of the praxis of charity derives from its connection with its origin and its objective. It comes from the gift of the Spirit, for which and by means of which the kingdom of God is realized. It is the force that causes the definitive kingdom to take shape among us in small, anticipatory signs. This, then, is not the final kingdom: charity lives on in the context of history. Its full comprehension, like the theological dimension as a whole, derives from the fact of Jesus Christ. It is he who reveals transcendence, the true service, the glory of the Father, the perfect realization of charity.

The Christological Dimension

In order to prepare trainees for spiritual discernment, during the second week of the Spiritual Exercises, Ignatius brings them in contact with the mysteries of the life of Jesus, in the hope that meditation will impregnate them little by little, by a kind of osmosis, with the very spirit of Christ. Their decisions will thus correspond to christological criteria. In this book we are attempting to see how these criteria may help us in choosing a concrete mediation for the political sphere.

A basic requirement here is to recognize the path that we must follow in elaborating christological criteria. In other words, it is important that we know what key of interpretation we will use to approach the gospels. Here we will not consider—because it has been definitively dealt with elsewhere—a simplistic approach to the gospels, literalism, a word-for-word application of the sayings of Christ to situations in our own day. Fundamentalist exegesis has been completely discredited by the teaching of the Catholic Church, beginning with the classic encyclical of Pius XII, *Divino Afflante Spiritu* (1943), the teachings of the Second Vatican Council (dogmatic constitution *Dei Verbum*), and the Pontifical Biblical Commission, originally established by Leo XIII in 1902, and restructured under the pontificate of Paul VI (1971).

Today it is taken for granted that any approach to the gospels must pass through the critical methods of form history, the history of traditions, and the history of redaction. In the process of selecting and studying a given mediation, there are various approaches to the text, each with its own emphasis that will influence the christological dimension of the discernment. We could mention a number of *polarities* in the interpretation of the gospels, each with its practical consequences for our topic. In order to highlight the dialectical aspect of the subject, we will single out the ones that best correspond to our situation.

Faith and History

One way of approaching the gospels is characterized by the tension between faith and history. Depending on which pole of interpretation prevails, the resulting christology will differ and will have a different effect on the criteria of discernment.

The approach in which the pole of *faith* is emphasized will be characterized by a perception of the historical Jesus in the light of christological elaboration, whether it derives from the New Testament itself or from later writings. The glorified Christ, the divine dimension of Jesus, provides the key for understanding how to gain access to the total Christ.

The foundation here is that Christ is Lord, that he is the Son of God, the divine Word. The suffering and struggles that he experienced in his earthly life were tests and trials through which he had to pass in order to enter into his glory (Luke 24:26). Everything becomes relative and receives its clarification from the resurrection, from the divine consciousness that Christ had of himself and of his mission. He knew the destiny that the Father alloted to him, and he fulfilled it along the path of obedience. His worthiness is to be seen precisely in his acceptance, his submission, his respect for the Father's eternal plan. He is the servant who is obedient unto death (Phil. 2:8; Rom. 5:19). This approach seeks to emphasize that which is permanent in Christ, his universal salvific significance, to which we relate by our faith in him.

The criteria that are elaborated on this basis are more susceptible to influence by factors antedating confrontation with the gospel. Doctrinal elaborations are profoundly conditioned by the doctrinal interests of the community that does the elaboration. These interests in turn obscure the interests rooted in the praxis of the community. A vicious circle results, from which it is impossible to escape without having recourse to a historical reinterpretation of Jesus, so as to provide criticism of the doctrinal and practical interests of the community that elaborated the dogmas.

An interpretation that starts with faith as the predominant element runs the risk of incorporating myths, which reveal prior, uncriticized options. They become criteria that are not controlled by a critical awareness. In particular, the determining interests of such elaborations are not clear-cut. They appeal all too readily to a divine providence, to a plan of God that is already given and must simply be implemented, whereas the elements of search, risk, and creation are made secondary. Passive aspects are emphasized: obedience, patience, submission, respect. This is most in harmony with the more sapiential stream of thought, at the expense of apocalyptic and prophetic viewpoints. When one is making a choice of mediations in the political realm, such a christological slant is not particularly helpful in the context of a social conflict such as our own.

The approach that emphasizes the *historical* aspect sees Jesus as someone who lived a concrete, unique, unrepeatable life. He did not live a "universal life," such as would exhaust all human possibilities. He lived within well-defined situations. In this sense, he cannot be "imitated." We make constant reference to his life story, so as not to transform it into myth. His significance is permanent and universal. He is the impulse and inspiration for our own life.

The historical aspect in Jesus has a double function in the elaboration of criteria. On the one hand, it does not permit a dogmatic universalization of the epical, unique, unrepeatable historical aspects of his Palestinian existence. Any direct, immediate imitation is bound to be ideologized. On the other hand, it is a reality to which we must have access in order to understand it in reference to our own situation and to allow ourselves to be called in question by it. We do not create the life of Jesus; we are questioned by it. To accomplish this, we need the twofold approach of discovering the structures of his life and understanding the meaning of this reality, by way of interrogating our own existence. His life challenges ours. It is a goading, unsettling reminder that does not allow us to be closed off into our own ideological circle.

For our context, that of conflict, this is the correct way to confront our criteria. This Jesus of Nazareth, in his deeds, prayers, attitudes, miracles, procedures, and relationships with the persons and social groups of his time, as also in his conduct with respect to Yahweh, religion, and the law, must be understood on the basis of all the possible cultural data that we can obtain—a task for exegesis—but not in the abstract. This approach is understood on the basis of our situation in the face of concrete mediations that we are to decide upon. In dialectical interaction it becomes the criterion, the dimension within which our discernment is determined.

This is not a cultural reinterpretation of the historical Jesus, such as would accommodate him to our own horizon and make him correspond to our own intellectual questionings. This is not a reconciliation of Jesus with "modern culture," with a new understanding of existence, or with current problems raised by science. Our concern here is with interpreting him as one who transforms a praxis into reality by questioning our own praxis. It is on this level that our question is posed. We find ourselves confronted by concrete mediations as a realization of our own praxis. And the Jesus of history, with the originality of his historical deeds, has the universal purpose of being for us the ultimate motivator and illuminator of our praxis.

The Jesus of history reveals himself to us in the role of a questioner in his relationship with the kingdom and within the eschatological horizon of his age. In his relationship with the kingdom a dialectic occurs that is very important in terms of our own discernment: the kingdom that comes to pass in the power of his miracles, of his word, and of his deeds is the kingdom that requires him to commit his life in his conflict with sin. On the one hand, Jesus acts as one who has fully realized the kingdom, who acts directly in making it come to pass among human beings. There is an impulse of "euphoria," of positiveness, that dominates Jesus' life. The enemy—evil in its varied physical, moral, and social forms, personified in the devil—appears to give way to his power. The kingdom of God is happening. Meanwhile, the radical force of evil is gradually becoming active in its continuous opposition to Jesus, to the point where he perceives that his own life is slipping away from him. There is a profound turning point in Jesus' activity, when his life begins to be dominated by an awareness of what will happen to the kingdom through the mediation of his *kenosis,* the gift of his life in a state of humility. Here is the dialectic of the kingdom as a work and as a gift. The Jesus of history does not allow us to absolutize either of these dimensions; in both cases it can lend itself easily to ideological manipulation.[80]

In the choice of mediations we must attend on the one hand to the dimension of the kingdom as a realization of Jesus' activity through the power of his miracles, his word, and his deeds. It is a very real dimension. The kingdom of God is also power—power in the sense of a struggle against the real enemies of humankind. In the cultural context of Jesus' life, these were expressed as sicknesses, as religious segregation, the marginalizing of sinners, the oppression of the law, and so forth. In our own context there are other manifestations. But the kingdom of God is realized to the extent that it carries on a battle to become victorious over such expressions of evil. The other dimension of the kingdom cannot be neglected: it is a gift. It requires us to make a gift of ourselves. It has its moments of silence, of obscurity, of apparent ineffectiveness, of weakness. It can be eclipsed by the enormity of the forces of evil. It may seem to be conquered, to be destroyed. But all the while it is like a seed. It grows in the warmth and moisture of the earth. It will spring forth in vigorous birth. It is an impulse of hope, of expectation, of a recoil strategy. The impulses differ. Both are necessary. The theory does not contain what is necessary to choose the manner of living them out. History meanders on, at one point offering opportunities for greater action and effectiveness, at others an opportunity for silence, waiting, and historical patience. The difficulty is in knowing how to live in this twofold pattern without giving way to exclusivism or arbitrary preferences.

Historical consideration of Jesus presents us with the difficult problem of discerning the significance of eschatology in his life and in our own. An understanding that reduces eschatology to its temporal aspect does not permit us to understand it properly. Whether for Jesus or for ourselves, it is not merely a matter of escaping from time, which would leave us merely with a sense of waiting, which has a negative influence on the value of our temporal actions. There is an anthropological dimension here that helps us to experience what humans make of the nearness of the eschaton, of "our ultimate concern" (Paul Tillich), of the final aspect of reality. An experience of this kind permits a variety of interpretations.

The eschatological happening is always present at any given moment, existentially thrusting persons in the world into a situation beyond the history of the world.[81] The eschatological event is the veiled future already proclaimed in promises, influencing the present through an awakened hope. Humanity stands in contradiction to the present reality of itself and the world. This contradiction gives birth to hope. Eschatology puts one in a critical position with respect to the present and induces a "reserved" attitude toward any temptation to absolutize present realities.[82]

Eschatology may be understood in the context of a liberating approach. In this sense, eschatology is the creative source of concrete pursuits and will become reality for the purpose of liberating humankind. It is not identified with such pursuits but instigates them, triggering partial, functional ideologies that will provide historical concretization of the liberation process, with all the fragility that characterizes human activities. It is not limited to a simple attitude of critical reserve but ventures forth into the world with concrete projects to verify the existence of liberation.

In the context of these thoughts, this ultimate understanding of eschatology as an instigator of projects has to conform to the standards of discernment. Eschatology becomes reality and is made concrete to the extent that the liberation of humankind is confirmed in the historical process. To paraphrase Ernst Bloch, we may say that *homo liberatus* is *Christus revelatus*. The end time of revelation, that moment at which history and eschatology become one *(Christus revelatus)*, will occur when humankind in its totality, both individually and as human society, is liberated *(homo liberatus)*. We are now living out that process. Christ is being revealed, and men and women are being liberated. To the extent that this liberation is taking place, to this extent Christ is being revealed. It is an eschatological process already underway, happening but not yet finished. This christological, eschatological criterion prompts us to choose those mediations that will transform such liberation into reality, because they are the agents that reveal Christ.

Christ: from God, to God

A second approach to the gospels has to do with the polarity of two differing points of view. The person of Christ may be interpreted either as an "epiphany of God" or as a "way to God." Here, of course, we are dealing with a matter of emphasis. Jesus is unquestionably both of these. But it is possible to interpret the gospels by emphasizing one viewpoint more than the other. This will influence the way in which we elaborate criteria.

The understanding of Christ as an *epiphany of God* brings us into a more contemplative, intellectual attitude toward Christ. It amounts to knowing God, to perceiving the being of God, by means of Christ. The figure of Christ occurs much more in its sense of complete reality, of the one who reveals the

Father, because he has an eternal intimacy with him.[83] As an epiphany of the Father, Christ is a model, an example to be imitated, the only possibility of gaining access to God. His words and his deeds give us a crystalization of revelation itself.

This way of understanding Christ, with its resulting interpretation of the gospel, approximates the interpretation that begins with the Christ of faith, which we have already examined. Its weak point is its idealistic, dogmatic, static nature. It appeals very much to the Greek mind. Totality is already given and predetermined, and all that remains for us is to get to know it.

On the contrary, if we regard Jesus as the *way to God,* then we will be led to emphasize the elements of search and risk. Jesus is, above all, someone who in his own life sought the will of the Father in the concrete contingencies of his own brief history. He experienced crises. He changed his models for understanding reality. He experimented with new strategies. He confronted powerful forces that involved him in the difficult interaction between advance and presence, on the one hand, and withdrawal and absence, on the other. Now he is appearing in public, confronting his enemies. He provokes them to anger with his questioning attitudes. But now he goes into hiding to devote himself to his disciples. And his life to the very end is this search for the will of the Father, this walking toward God. And in this he becomes our access to the Father, via the same paths. It is not the clearness of revelations that he imparts to us but this constant striving, this perpetual questioning.

For our choice of criteria, the first key to interpretation centers more on the aspect of clarity, security, and certainty as to the will of God. The second, by contrast, helps us see that the christological dimension is not going to settle a question or establish a proof, but is going to leave us in a constant, searching uncertainty. It is by this process that we gain access to God. And the mediations that we choose will be christologically coherent to the extent that they are adopted in an attitude of searching, of striving, of a constant overcoming—the very process that Jesus himself underwent in his historical life. He is not the road already traveled; he is the call to take the road. He is not a treasure trove of self-evident truths, but a call and a challenge.

This brings us to a better understanding of our historical process. Access to God is through Christ. And it is particularly evident in the life of Jesus that his walk toward the Father coincides with his task of living and sharing life with others in an effort to create a human community and a human solidarity where religious, political, and ideological conflicts are overcome by the greater force of righteousness and reconciliation. Jesus died performing that task. He did not finish it; he left it open. The christological criterion is clearly seen as an index of the mediations that give us access to God via human fellowship and the solidarity of our deeper interests.

Socio-Political Factors

A third approach to the gospels confronts us with still another polarity. Here we see more clearly the socio-political conditions that affect our choice.

On the one hand, Christ is seen as the "fulfilment" of human reality. In this view, Christic structures have left their mark on the world and on history. History is his revelation, his fulfilment. This is a basically positive concept of human reality. It came as a reaction to a completely negative, Jansenistic stream of thought, tainted with Manichaeism, which had come to dominate the hermeneutics of traditional Catholicism. Influenced in particular by Teilhard de Chardin, a modern christological interpretation of scripture emphasizes the historical procession toward the Omega Point.

This interpretation satisfies those thinkers living in a world where enormous economic, political, and ideological contradictions are not perceived in all their intensity. These are theologians who live in abundance, where sin is committed in a context of excessive abundance and may be corrected simply by an interior renewal. Here is a christology where the elements of the neocapitalist system are viewed in a marriage of freedom with material abundance. Christ is seen as the one who "fulfils" this beautiful wedding. The "dangerous" aspect of this abundance of consumer goods is sanctified by its "christification." It is the expression of the wealth of Christ that has become history, in which we are called to participate.

This type of christological interpretation will be sensitive to reformist mediations that aim at a high appraisal of the products of human labor. The "fulfilment" mentality sacralizes these goods only by disregarding the social conditions in which they are produced. But here labor is seen as something in its own right and not as simply another factor in the social relationships of production. It is not understood in terms of buying and selling, where the human element is degraded, but in its significance of constructing the universe, transforming the world, participating as co-creators in the work of God himself.

The other polar alternative sees Christ as the cross, a criticism, a disclosure of contradictions and of the visceral sin of the human condition. There are conflicts that cannot be avoided or overlooked. Jesus during his earthly existence was a restless unveiler of such contradictions. He did not come to do a cover-up job or to "fulfil" reality as the historical harvest of so many profound injustices. Social relationships constitute a factor that cannot be ignored in understanding the world, and in particular the activity of Christ. From Jesus' criticism a new person and a new society emerge. From death, from crucifixion, and from their contradictions, a newness is born, not just a linear fulfilment of an already existent reality.

The death of Jesus is not understood as a sacralized event for its own sake, as a negation of life, or even as a simple expression of giving. It must be historically recovered and viewed in relationship with the concrete life of Jesus. He died because he pointed out the contradictions of the social milieu in which he lived. It is not just the death of someone who saves us and becomes a standard. It is the death of Jesus; it is the death of the man who pointed out, in the historical context of his life, terrible cruelties, deceitfulness, lying, social injustice, and ideological imposition. The death of Jesus is the supreme revelation of the contradictions to be found in reality. He instituted a radical and final rupture within human reality. He demonstrated that the way of injustice and exploitation is impervious and irreformable. It must be crucified so that it may come to life in the newness of resurrection and not in a linear continuity of "fulfilment."[84]

An interpretation of this type quite naturally leads us to elaborate still another class of criteria. The christological dimension is now seen as a criticism of those ingenuous mediations that do not address the conflictual aspect of reality. It unmasks a false optimism based on mediations that take place at the expense of exploited human beings. It will demonstrate that one dare not choose mediations that "fulfil," that re-form reality, but those that become its "cross," crucifying the seeds of its injustice and plucking up the deep roots of its exploitation.

In a word, the christological dimension should provide us with criteria that help us to achieve a real liberation and not just an orthodox understanding of reality. We may elaborate criteria that point to the more intellectual interests of a hermeneutic situated within orthodoxy, or to interests concerned with the transformation of reality. It will be our choice of "lenses" that will determine the way in which christological criteria are elaborated. The christological dimension is not a pre-existing assumption, totally independent of our comprehension. It is controlled by this basic choice of the type of christology we wish to elaborate.

In our Latin American context there can be no doubt that the paths we are to take point more in the direction of a historical interpretation of the gospels, of the understanding of Jesus as the way to God, and as a critique of the reality in which we live our lives. Our set of criteria must be situated on this side of the christological divide in order to choose concrete mediations.

The Ecclesiological Dimension

Unquestionably, there is no such thing as a spiritual discernment that does not recognize the normative role of the church. We are the church, and no choice of a mediation can ignore this dimension. St. Ignatius elaborated the classical rules for "being in tune with the church." A preoccupation with the ecclesial dimension of choices dominates the entire process of discernment.

There has been an enormous change in the cultural context, of course. Ignatius lived during the painful beginnings of the Reformation. He created a very rigid intraecclesiastical spirit, to resist the impact of Luther's liberal ideas. We now live in a climate of ecumenism, of "ecclesiastical détente." Today's spirit is less defensive when called into question. We actually feel the need of being called into question, so strong is our suspicion that we might easily become involved with ideologies foreign to the gospel. The ecclesial dimension will no longer have the rigidity it had in Ignatius's day. Nevertheless there is a *spirit* that remains the same, making it necessary for us to identify its form of expression in the present context. We shall attempt to grasp the significance of this ecclesial dimension as it applies to our discernment of political mediations.

Perhaps one of the most important changes that has taken place is that of understanding the church more as *mission* than as *institution*. The criteria of discernment must keep in mind all the interests of the church, and not so much those of orthodoxy as those of praxis. The main interest is not the church for its own sake, in defense of the institution, but in the people it seeks to serve. I define "ecclesial" not in the sense of "ecclesiastical" but in the sense of "oriented to the people of God." "Ecclesiastical" derives its meaning from "ecclesial," from what belongs to the church—that is, the people of God. This is the church's primary responsibility.

The ecclesial dimension of the criteria for discernment leads us to be directly concerned with everything that helps to build the community of Christians. Any mediation that does not, when applied, help the people of God to grow must be excluded on the basis of this criterion. Unfortunately the ecclesial dimension has all too often been restricted to a comparison between the mediation and the doctrine of the church. In such cases one forgets that the doctrine in question is not a "self-evident truth," independent of pastoral practice and the bedrock experience of the church.

If we accept the practice of the church as the basic criterion, then we enter a field where pluralism becomes more evident and the universality of the criteria takes on a sense of inspiration rather than of normativeness. The needs and requirements of an ecclesial community will vary considerably according to their latitude and longitude. Although pluralism is present, it is not to be allowed to degenerate into a facile relativism, because the needs are very concrete and frequently quite apparent. The difficulty in our reasoning is that many problems and alternatives arise at the theoretical level, but in concrete practice the solutions are considerably simpler.

In the Latin American context, the Medellín option points us to a new conception of the mission of the church. The statements of Paul VI in his opening address to the Second General Conference of the Latin American Bishops (1968) reveal his awareness of living at a unique moment, a time of "total reflection," when "the future calls for effort, daring, and sacrifice, which introduces a deep anxiety into the Church."[85]

There is an awareness that a new note has been sounded in our Latin American church. With this has arisen a new self-consciousness in the church that has become a historical criterion for our discernment. This new self-consciousness is manifested by the church's effort to be a presence in the current transformation of the continent, addressing its attentions to the poor, the oppressed, and those who yearn for liberation. Latin America is in a stage of transformation that is going to happen with or without the presence of the church. Its only choice is whether it intends to be present or not. At Medellín the Latin American bishops chose, in the name of their churches, to be a church that is active in this transformation.

This ecclesial perspective is of decisive importance for our criteria of discernment. Any mediation that does not reflect such a presence cannot be regarded as viable for the church. On the contrary, any historical or political concretization that expresses and actualizes a liberating presence within the process of transformation going on on this continent will have behind it the weight of the Latin American church. St. Ignatius's "being in tune with the church" takes on a fresh nuance of meaning in the present context. For Ignatius, the phrase meant "confessing one's sins to a priest, the religious vows, celibacy, honoring the relics of the saints, the way of the cross, religious pilgrimages, indulgences, jubilees, votive candles."[86] Many of the things that Ignatius honored are practices we no longer recognize. If we reinterpret his rules, we will honor "those mediations that signify the presence of the church in the transformations of our continent according to the spirit of Medellín."

Theology and the magisterium of the church have carried their reflections beyond Medellín, seeking to deepen its basic insights and trends. We could refer in particular to the Synods of 1971 and 1974, and all that they indicated as material for preparation and further reflection. The Synod of 1971 dealt directly with the problem of justice in the world, in its final document on this subject.[87] The Synod of 1974, which began with the subject of evangelization in today's world, provided a wealth of reflections for this new ecclesial consciousness. In his Apostolic Exhortation *Evangelii Nuntiandi* of December 8, 1975, Paul VI officially adopted quite a number of features that had been added while the Synod was being prepared and held.

Thus we are unable to formulate a set of criteria within the ecclesial dimension without being inspired and imbued with this line of theological reflection. It is important to remember that our discernment will be "in tune with the church" to the extent that it responds to this perception of the church as revealed in the recent magisterial documents of the pope, the Synods, and the Latin American bishops.[88]

This new ecclesial consciousness has not been without its tensions with ideologies that have characterized previous conceptions, on the one hand, and which threaten to smother the new.[89] The tension and the battle lines operate on the twofold level of theory and practice. There is still stiff resistance to the concepts articulated at Medellín and in the follow-up documents. It actually seems as though the church is taking steps backward, unwilling to assimilate the elements proposed by the above-mentioned documents. There is nothing strange about this. A certain mentality is not immediately transformed by a mere writing or reading of documents. Many authors do not themselves perceive the purpose of everything they are writing or to which they subscribe. And so there is a pulling back. This mentality is slowly being consolidated in some sectors and is losing ground in others. It is all part of the phenomenon of the ebb and flow of historical movements.

There is another time lag between the elaboration of theory and the practice of the church. Thus it is easy to see why these setbacks and discontinuities are so prominent. To put these elements into practice requires a considerable amount of change, for which the church is unprepared, and this is why it is not in the forefront in adopting decisions that have been made.

For our situation, all that is needed is to emphasize the importance of this new ecclesial consciousness in the elaboration of criteria for discernment. It sets us free from the perplexity caused by regional decisions of this or that member of the hierarchy. There are many who try to take refuge in a supposedly neutral attitude of the church toward mediations with a political intent. This new ecclesial consciousness is precisely what will call this attitude into account as not being "in tune with the church." There is a danger that we will identify with a reality that goes beyond the dimension of the church and make this the criterion of discernment, based on particular, concrete decisions of this or that bishop. It is important that we keep in contact with the entire mainstream of the church, with an awareness of all the theological and pastoral data made available to us. This is a valid option and is being adopted more and more by the Latin American church as a whole.

Summary

Criteria of discernment are not to be regarded as a codification, arranged in a rigid sequence. As we have seen, it is rather a perspective that we must create, and a critical capacity for properly perceiving our own existential situation. Thus we are not looking for a book of recipes whose application in discerning reality is thought to have a well-defined result. To continue in this way would be to feed the delusion that we are capable of clearly defining God's plans for us. We have a deep-down desire to enjoy a degree of certainty that Christ himself did not possess.

Criteria are to be used in such a way as to show us the path that we must take. We seek to exercise a critical vigilance over the improper interventions of disguised ideologies. We will maintain a certain suspicion regarding current statements, in the form of spiritual precepts, that perform the function of criteria for choices. Discernment is a process of critical clarification and thus requires criteria that attempt to perform the role of making such awareness available. In particular, it is opposed to the facile use of spiritual principles disconnected from their concrete context and highly vulnerable to the manipulations of various interests.

In the context of the discernment process, criteria are understood as an internal feature of the process itself. They do not sit outside the process as judges but themselves constitute a dimension of the act of discernment. If we single them out so explicitly, it is for didactic reasons. The very spirit that pervades the discernment process from the beginning, whether in the creation of prerequisites or in the structuring of the act of discernment, is what will determine the elaboration and understanding of the criteria. Here is a unique process whose ultimate goal is to read into a given concrete reality the signs of the will of God. For this "reading" to be reliable, it must conform to a series of conditions. The elaboration of discernment criteria has sought to analyze these conditions.

The dialectical, synthetic interplay of subjective and objective criteria permits us to operate in a climate of honesty, realism, and a theological, christological, and ecclesiological spirit. This is our task in the reading of God's presence in the world around us. It is this for which we are responsible. The errors and complications that still overtake us pertain to our historical situation. They cannot be totally avoided but can be continually examined, to the extent that we regard discernment as a process and not as a set of established definitions.

Conclusion

In concluding this series of reflections, it seems to us that three things have been made clear: the importance of the political dimension in seeking and realizing the will of God, its complexity, and its relationship to faith.

Politics is fundamental. We live with human beings in a context that is very concrete. There are innumerable forces interacting, there are a variety and an antagonism of interests. We may skirt around them in our decisions, but it will only be out of ignorance, because in reality we are participants in this interplay. We cannot escape this inevitability. Our apostolic works, our deeds form part of the concrete framework of history. We are not interested in measuring the importance of our actions. What is basic is to become aware of our responsibility and the impossibility of fleeing from this "presence." We must respond with all the seriousness and enlightenment of our participation in history. The Lord will hold us accountable, not for the number of talents, but for the way we use them (Matt. 25:14–30). The talents are not just our attributes but also the historical opportunities and the social intent of our actions. Even if we are poor in human gifts, our life can still speak in actions that reach a goal far beyond our human smallness.

At this moment, our responsibility looms large in the kingdom of God. We cannot be satisfied with fleeing to an inner battle line of good intentions. We are responsible for the concrete outcome of our presence or absence, of our action or failure to act. The more significant our position in the political arena, often independent of what we wish or intend, the more discernment is required as to the positions we take.

Politics is becoming increasingly more complex. A simplistic, spur-of-the-moment interpretation is bound to be incorrect. Such an interpretation is generally in agreement with the dominant interests that monopolize the information and social analysis systems. If we do not question our spontaneous interpretation, then we are implicitly accepting the rules of the game written by the powerful. And there is no guarantee that the game is being played in a manner consistent with the kingdom of God. On the contrary, we have good reason to suspect that the kingdom has quite divergent interests. It is more closely related to persons who are on the margin of society. "In the Bible," observes Carlos Mesters, "there is one constant factor that stands out: from Abraham all the way to the New Testament, it is always in the margin that the voice of God takes on its form, content, and meaning. In times of crisis and renewal, it is from the 'margin' that God begins to call out his people and to recover the relevance and dynamism from which they have strayed."[90] Are things any different today? Or is God still revealing his plans to us through the lowliness of the weak?

What this means is that in order to be sensitive to this hushed voice we should not rely upon an immediate reading of realty, which is so often seen through the spectacles of the powerful. Our task, then, is to penetrate with our discernment to the complexity of the situation, so that our decisions will not confirm interests that are opposed to those we are pursuing in the name of the kingdom. Our thinking will need to reflect this complexity and to help us see with greater clarity those mediations that are more compatible with the evangelical dimension.

The significance of politics first comes through to us in our understanding of the faith. Politics and faith have a close relationship. It is a relationship that does not depend upon our political awareness but on the common implications of these two factors. Our awareness discovers and unveils what is actually happening. Woe to those of us who do not perceive it, because our faith is thus alienated rather than being transformed into a force that builds the kingdom of God. What is important is the kingdom and not the pettiness of our own interests. Hence we need to apply ourselves seriously to the task of discernment, even though it may be complex and difficult. It is not easy to have clear vision. This does not excuse us from putting forth the effort to analyze reality and confront this analysis with the gospel.

Discernment does not preclude the possibility that our decisions are going to be limited and provisional. On the contrary, it assumes that human mediations are fragile and that our own knowledge is limited. Thus we need to put forth the effort to think, so that by means of this very temporality we may trace the contours of the kingdom of God. There are events that have already happened in history, that have left their tracks upon it, but there is a final form that has not yet been filled out. It is in this time between the "now" and the "not yet," the age of the church, that we are appointed to live. We are invited to participate with all our faculties in building the kingdom through these provisional and precarious choices of ours.

The limitations imposed upon our choices does not excuse us from the responsibility of discernment. On the contrary, these are what urge us to become participants in the interplay. Our life is a risk. Risk consists of freedom and responsibility. Freedom is our basic capacity for self-determination. Responsibility makes us aware of this basic dimension of our existence. The alternatives are to abdicate, to evade, to come up with a neurotic solution to the problem, or to run the risk.

Abdicating from the process of discernment can be seen at the psychological level as an attempt to reverse the process of individualization, by fleeing from the risk of assuming our own identity, freedom, and autonomy, though not intending to reverse it by a tendency to domination, to destruction, or to automatic submission and conformity. All of these are formulas that seek to resolve ambiguously the relationship we have with the world, with history, and with other persons. Valid formulas are in line with the concepts of love, politics, work, transformation of reality, and involvement in the historical process.[91] At the level of socio-political analysis such an abdication may be the result of uncriticized ideological involvements, defending unarticulated and unconfessed interests. There will always be a suspicion of impurity, whether psychological or ideological.

Discernment becomes especially important at this point in the life of the church. In the past a simple, straightforward recourse to precise statements precluded a more laborious effort in order to be "in tune with the church" in our decision-making. Today pluralism is so prevalent within the church that such recourse is seldom possible. We find ourselves going around in a circle. The ecclesial dimension calls for ecclesial discernment. Even ecclesial tradition, properly so-called, is subject to a wide diversity of interpretation within the church.

The problem becomes even more complicated in the area of the relationships between faith and politics, because so many interests of another nature are involved. In the concrete world where decisions are made, these interests mingle with theological and ecclesiastical elements in such a way that discernment is made difficult but no less necessary.

Even a rapid scanning of documents and statements by organizations and persons connected with church institutions gives us some idea of the complexity and diversity of positions held on decisions of political import. This applies not only to individual cases where interpretations tend to multiply, but also in areas of pastoral activity, where the scope is considerably wider. The very documents that are intended to articulate the position of the church on concrete issues are subject to an editing process that reshapes and amends them to such an extent that in the end they provide no clear orientation. The result is that in the process of discernment both the circumstances and the system of elaboration must be considered so that we do not end up relying on pat formulas that are more a pattern of compromise than of a clear line of action.

Because of all the complexity of this situation, which cannot be easily perceived and yet requires us to take some position, we are more and more called upon to exercise discernment in the field of politics. It is thus possible for us to maintain a vigilant, critical awareness, constantly called into account by the word of God, in such a way that our decisions may more readily correspond to the demands of the present moment.

Discernment in contemporary politics is a need of such importance that failure to engage in it is an omission that is becoming increasingly serious in its consequences. Only by adopting this process can we live up to what is expected of a Christian and a religious. Let us hope that future generations will not rise up to denounce us for our failing to be clear or for failing to have a really Christian spirit. It is only by a serious involvement in socio-politico-economic analysis of reality, together with a sincere reading of the gospels, that we can be sure we are making decisions that are Christian and enlighted.

Notes

1. Paul Ricoeur, *Histoire et verité* (Paris: Seuil, 1955), p. 165. Eng., *History and Truth,* trans. C.L. Kelbley (Evanston: Northwestern University Press, 1965).
2. Paul Ricoeur, "Le paradoxe politique," *Esprit* 25 (1957) 721-45.
3. "Os Cristãos e a política," *SEDOC* 5 (1972-73), col. 1389-1408.
4. "Eu ouvi os clamores do meu povo," document issued by the bishops and religious superiors of the Brazilian Northeast, *SEDOC* 6 (1973-74), col. 607-28.
5. O. Dana, *Os deuses dançantes: Un estudo dos cursilhos de cristandade* (Petrópolis: Vozes, 1975), pp. 84, 151, and esp. 133-62, where the author analyzes psychosocial, religious, and politico-sociological functions of the Cursillos.
6. J. B. Libânio, *Revista Eclesiástica Brasileira (REB)* 33 (1973) 139-54, 391-411.
7. Louis Althusser and Etienne Balabar, *Lire le Capital* (Paris: Maspéro, 1968), p. 115. Eng., *Reading Capital,* trans. Ben Brewster (New York: Pantheon, 1970), p. 93.
8. M. de Certeau, *L'opération historique* (Paris, 1974), p. 15.
9. L. Goldmann, *Marxisme et sciences humaines* (Paris: Gallimard, 1970), pp. 121-22.
10. These reflections are inspired by J. L. Segundo, *Liberación de la teología* (Buenos Aires-Mexico City: Carlos Lohlé, 1975), pp. 11-45. Eng., *The Liberation of Theology* (Maryknoll, N.Y.: Orbis, 1976), pp. 7-9, 39-56.
11. See M. de Certeau, "La relation à l'Etranger," in *L'opération historique;* Henrique de Lima Voz, *Cristianismo-Cultura; Fé-Linguagem,* 3rd series (Rio de Janeiro: Centro João XXIII, n.d.).
12. Alvin Toffler, *Future Shock* (New York: Random House, 1970; Bantam, 1971), pp. 306-7.
13. J. M. Casabo, "Discernimiento cristiano y opciones políticas," in *Fe y Política* (Buenos Aires: Guadalupe, 1973), p. 156.
14. Leonardo Boff, *A vida religiosa e a Igreja no processo de libertacão,* Vida Religiosa, Temas Atuais, n. 1 (Petrópolis-Rio de Janeiro: Vozes-CRB, 1975), pp. 85-101.
15. Clodovis Boff, *Théologie et libération: Questions d'épistémologie* (doctoral dissertation, Catholic University of Louvain, 1976), pp. 421 ff.; J. B. Libânio, "Criterios de Autenticidade do Catholicismo," *REB* 36 (1976) 71-72.
16. Juan Alfaro, *Esperanza cristiana y liberación del hombre* (Barcelona: Herder, 1972), p. 24.

17. Rubem Alves, *A Theology of Human Hope* (New York: Corpus, 1969).
18. René Laurentin, *Nouvelles dimensions de l'espérance* (Paris: Cerf, 1972), pp. 11 ff.
19. See J. Stierli, "Das Ignatianische Gebet: Gott suchen in allen dingen," in F. Wulf, ed., *Ignatius von Loyola. Seine geistliche Gestalt und sein Vermächtnis* (Würzburg, 1956), pp. 151-82.
20. D. Gil, "Discernimiento y liberación," *Stromata* 28 (1972) 322.
21. R. Antoncich, "Dimensión social de los Ejercicios Espirituales," *Cuaderno de Espiritualidad* 1 (Lima, 1975), pp. 5-6.
22. J. Aldunate, "El concepto de 'Política' y su significación para los religiosos," *Testimonio* 21-22 (Santiago, 1973), p. 26.
23. "Le Marxisme," *Chronique Sociale de France* (Lyons, 1970).
24. Karl Marx, *Oeuvres,* II, La Pléiade (Paris: NRF, 1968).
25. J. Deratz and A. Nocent, *Dizionario dei Testi Conciliari* (Brescia: Queriniana, 1966); the term appears in at least thirty paragraphs; see also Christian Duquoc, *Christologie, I: Le Messie* (Paris: Cerf, 1972), p. 239.
26. Duquoc, *Le Messie,* p. 240.
27. José Comblin, "The National Security Doctrine," in *The Church and the National Security State* (Maryknoll, N.Y.: Orbis 1979), pp. 64-78.
28. Casabo, "Discernimiento cristiano," p. 154.
29. José Comblin, "La nueva práctica de la Iglesia en el sistema de la Seguridad Nacional. Exposicion de sus principios téoricos," in *Encuentro Latino-americano de Teología: Liberación y Cautiverio* (Mexico City, 1976), p. 156.
30. Ricoeur, "La paradoxe politique," p. 730.
31. René Coste, *Les dimensions politiques de la foi* (Paris: Ouvrières, 1972), pp. 37-38.
32. P. Fernandez, "Criterios para ayudar a definir la actitud del religioso frente a la política," in *Testimonio* 21-22 (1973) 23; CLAR, "Vida religiosa e compromisso sócio-político," *SEDOC* 8 (1976), col. 851-80.
33. Enrique Dussel, "Sobre la historia de la teología en América Latina," in *Encuentro Latino-americano de Teología: Liberación y Cautiverio,* pp. 19-20.
34. F. Taborda, "Teologia e Ciências no Diálogo Interdisciplinar," *REB* 34 (1974) 833.
35. Clodovis Boff, dissertation *Théologie et libération;* these reflections owe much to his excellent work.
36. Taborda, "Teologia e Ciências," p. 828.
37. Dussel, "Sobre la historia de la teología," p. 20.
38. Paul Lazarsfeld, *Qu'est-ce que ce la Sociologie?* (Paris: Gallimard, 1971), pp. 106-24.
39. R. Antoncich, "Los Ejercicios y el discerimiento espiritual de las opciones políticas," *Cuaderno de Espiritualidad* 2 (Lima, 1975) 2 ff.
40. J. Mancini, *Teologia, Ideologia, Utopia* (Brescia: Queriniana, 1974), pp. 266 ff.

41. Henrique de Lima Vaz, "A Grande Mensagem de SS. João XXIII," *Síntese Política, Econômica, Social* 5 (1963) 19.
42. N. Poulantzas, *Pouvoir politique et classes sociales de l'Etat capitaliste, Textes à appui* (Paris: Maspéro, 1968), pp. 224-25.
43. J. B. Libânio, "Evangelização e Ideologia," *Convergência* 8 (1975) 623-35.
44. CRB, 1977, "XI Assembléia Geral Ordinária Eletiva," I, *Convergência* 9 (1976) 265.
45. CRB, 1977, "XI Assembléia Geral," II, 323-31.
46. CRB, 1977, "XI Assembléia Geral," III, 451-58.
47. Taborda, "Teologia e Ciências," pp. 824-38.
48. M. Lenz, "O desinvolvimento brasileiro; Características e implicações de um modelo," in *Evangelização no Brasil, hoje: conteùdo e linguagem* (São Paulo: Loyola, 1976), p. 18.
49. Peter Berger, *An Invitation to Sociology: A Humanist Perspective* (New York: Doubleday-Anchor, 1963), p. 23.
50. Segundo, *Liberation of Theology*, pp. 91-95, 100.
51. Karl Marx, *Contribution à la critique de la Philosophie du Droit de Hegel* (Paris, 1971), pp. 52-53. Eng., "Contributions to the Critique of Hegel's Philosophy of Right," in Karl Marx, *Early Writings*, trans. T. B. Bottomore (New York: McGraw-Hill, 1964), pp. 43-44.
52. For all Marx's objections to the social principles of Christianity, see *Marx-Engels Gesamtausgabe* (MEGA), I, 6, 278, quoted in H. Niel, *Karl Marx, Situation du Marxisme* (Paris: DDB, 1971), p. 233.
53. St. Augustine, *Confessions*, XIII, 9-10.
54. J. B. Libânio, *Vida Religiosa e Testemunho Público* (Rio de Janeiro: CRB, 1971).
55. *SEDOC* 8 (1976), col. 851-80.
56. Document of the Plenary Session of the Bishops of France, October 28, 1972, cited by Fernandez, "Criterios," *Testimonio* 22-23 (1973) 30.
57. P. Valadier, *Essais sur la modernité. Nietzsche et Marx* (Paris: Cerf-Desclée, 1974), pp. 9-32.
58. J. Aldunate, "El Concepto de 'Política'," *Testimonio* 22-23 (1973) 27.
59. Karl Rahner, "Ignatianische Frömmigkeit und Herz-Jesu-Verehrung," in *Sendung und Gnade* (Innsbruck-Vienna-Munich: Tyrolia, 1959), pp. 520-22. Eng., *Mission and Grace* III (London-New York: Sheed & Ward, 1965).
60. Henrique de Lima Vaz, "O problema atual da hermenêutica," manuscript (Belo Horizonte, 1973).
61. Joseph Ratzinger, "Bemerkungen zur Frage der Charismen in der Kirche," in *Die Zeit Jesu. Festschrift für H. Schlier*, Günther Bornkamm and Karl Rahner, eds. (Freiburg-Basel-Vienna: Herder, 1970), pp. 267-69.
62. Oscar Cullmann, *Cristo e Política* (Rio de Janeiro, 1963); idem, *Jesus and the Revolutionaries*, trans. Gareth Putnam (New York: Harper & Row, 1970), p. 50; M. Hengel, *Foi Jesus Revolucionário?* (Petrópolis: Vozes, 1971), Eng.: *Was Jesus a*

Revolutionist? (Philadelphia: Fortress, 1971); C. Boff, "Foi Jesus Revolucionário?," *REB* 31 (1971) 97-118.

63. Carlos Mesters, *Palavra de Deus na história dos homens,* II (Petrópolis: Vozes, 1971), pp. 133-81; J. L. Segundo, *Masas y minorías en la dialética divina de la liberación* (Buenos Aires: La Aurora, 1973), pp. 58-62.

64. N. Werneck Sodré, *Fundamentos do materialismo histórico* (Rio de Janeiro: Ed. Civ. Bras., 1968), pp. 113 ff.

65. Hugo Assmann, "Political Commitment in the Context of the Class Struggle," *Concilium* 84 (1973); idem, *Political Commitment and the Christian Community,* Alois Muller and Norbert Greinacher, eds. (New York: Herder & Herder, 1973), p. 95.

66. Segundo, *Masas y minorías;* idem, *The Liberation of Theology,* pp. 208-40.

67. J. Freud, "Les politiques du salut," *Le Point Théologique* 10 (Paris, 1974) 9-22.

68. Thomas Luckmann, *The Invisible Religion: The Problem of Religion in Modern Society* (New York: Macmillan, 1967).

69. Dana, *Os deuses dançantes,* p. 152.

70. J. van Nieuwenhove, "Les Théologies de la Libération latino-américaines," *Le Point Théologique* 10 (Paris: Beauchesne, 1974) 98.

71. J. C. Scannone, "O desafio atual à linguagem teológica latino-americana sobre libertação," *Síntese* 1 (1974, new series), 2-20.

72. Comblin, "La Nueva Práctica," pp. 155-76.

73. Ibid., p. 175.

74. These reflections are based on elements of the sociology of knowledge, especially as found in the works of Peter Berger.

75. Henrique de Lima Vaz, "Discrição e amor. A propósito da 'Eleição' inaciana nos Exercícios, " *Verbum* 13 (1956) 479 ff.

76. R. Mehl, "La crise actuelle de la Théologie," *Etudes Théologiques* 45 (1970) 355-66.

77. De Lima Vaz, "Discrição e amor," p. 169.

78. See Z. Alszeghy and M. Flick, "Gloria Dei," *Gregorianum* 36 (1955) 361-90; idem, *Il Creatore. L'inizio della salvezza* (Florence: Fiorentina, 1961), pp. 126 ff.

79. José Comblin, *Théologie de la révolution* (Paris: Ed. Universitaires, 1970), pp. 230-31; idem, *Théologie de la pratique révolutionnaire* (Paris: Ed. Universitaires, 1974), pp. 54-61.

80. Jon Sobrino, "Tesis Sobre una Cristología histórica," *ECA* 30 (1975) 457-82.

81. Rudolf Bultmann, "Histoire et Eschatologie dans le Nouveau Testament" (1954), in *Foi et Compréhension, II. Eschatologie et Démythologisation* (Paris: Seuil, 1969), pp. 112-28.

82. Jürgen Moltmann, *Theologie der Hoffnung* (Munich, 1966). Eng., *The Theology of Hope* (New York: Harper & Row, 1967), p. 88.

83. Juan Alfaro, "Cristo glorioso, Revelador del Padre," in *Cristología y Antropología* (Madrid, 1973), pp. 141-82.

84. Duquoc, *Le Messie,* pp. 19-69.

85. Pope Paul VI, Allocution at the Second General Conference of Latin American Bishops (Medellín, 1968), *The Church in the Present-Day Transformation of Latin America in the Light of the Council: Conclusions,* Louis Colonnese, ed. (Washington: Latin American Bureau of the USCC, 1968), p. 20.

86. St. Ignatius Loyola, *Spiritual Exercises,* trans. Lewis Delmagé, S. J. (New York: Wagner, 1968), pp. 170-72; on "thinking [being in tune] with the church," see. nn. 352-70; on relics, indulgences, etc., see n. 358.

87. Synod of 1971, "Justice in the World," in *The Gospel of Peace and Justice: Catholic Social Teaching since Pope John,* presented by Joseph Gremillion (Maryknoll, N.Y.: Orbis, 1976), pp. 513-29.

88. J. B. Libânio, "Elaboração do conceito de Igreja Particular," in *Igreja Particular* (São Paulo: Loyola, 1974), pp. 41 ff.

89. R. Muñoz, *Nueva Conciencia de la Iglesia en América Latina* (Santiago: Nueva Universidad, 1973).

90. Carlos Mesters, "O futuro do nosso passado," *SEDOC* 7 (1974-75), col. 1136.

91. J. B. Libânio, "Compromisso perpétuo ou temporário?," *Convergência* 9 (1976), 464-76.

www.ingramcontent.com/pod-product-compliance
Lightning Source LLC
Chambersburg PA
CBHW072154160426
43197CB00012B/2377